TERENCE RATTIGAN

Born in 1911, a scholar at Harrow and at Trinity College, Oxford, Terence Rattigan had his first long-running hit in the West End at the age of twenty-five: *French Without Tears* (1936). His next play, *After the Dance* (1939), opened to euphoric reviews yet closed under the gathering clouds of war, but with *Flare Path* (1942) Rattigan embarked on an almost unbroken series of successes, with most plays running in the West End for at least a year and several making the transition to Broadway: *While the Sun Shines* (1943), *Love in Idleness* (1944), *The Winslow Boy* (1946), *The Browning Version* (performed in double-bill with *Harlequinade*, 1948), *Who is Sylvia?* (1950), *The Deep Blue Sea* (1952), *The Sleeping Prince* (1953) and *Separate Tables* (1954). From the mid-fifties, with the advent of the 'Angry Young Men', he enjoyed less success on stage, though *Ross* (1960) and *In Praise of Love* (1973) were well received. As well as seeing many of his plays turned into successful films, Rattigan wrote a number of original plays for television from the fifties onwards. He was knighted in 1971 and died in 1977.

T0346958

**Other titles by the same author
published by Nick Hern Books**

After the Dance

The Browning Version and *Harlequinade*

Cause Célèbre

The Deep Blue Sea

First Episode

Flare Path

French Without Tears

In Praise of Love

Love in Idleness / Less Than Kind

Rattigan's Nijinsky
(adapted from Rattigan's screenplay by Nicholas Wright)

Separate Tables

The Winslow Boy

Terence Rattigan

WHO IS SYLVIA?
and
DUOLOGUE

Introduced by
Dan Rebellato

NICK HERN BOOKS
London
www.nickhernbooks.co.uk

A Nick Hern Book

This edition of *Who is Sylvia?* and *Duologue* first published in Great Britain in 2011 as a paperback original by Nick Hern Books Limited, 14 Larden Road, London W3 7ST. *Who is Sylvia?* was first published in 1951 by Hamish Hamilton Ltd. *Duologue* is published here for the first time.

Typeset by Nick Hern Books, London
Printed in the UK by Mimeo Ltd, Huntingdon, Cambridgeshire PE29 6XX

A CIP catalogue record for this book is available from the British Library

ISBN 978 1 84842 165 3

Terence Rattigan (1911–1977)

Terence Rattigan stood on the steps of the Royal Court Theatre, on 8 May 1956, after the opening night of John Osborne's *Look Back in Anger*. Asked by a reporter what he thought of the play, he replied, with an uncharacteristic lack of discretion, that it should have been retitled 'Look how unlike Terence Rattigan I'm being.'[1] And he was right. The great shifts in British theatre, marked by Osborne's famous premiere, ushered in kinds of playwriting which were specifically unlike Rattigan's work. The pre-eminence of playwriting as a formal craft, the subtle tracing of the emotional lives of the middle classes – those techniques which Rattigan so perfected – fell dramatically out of favour, creating a veil of prejudice through which his work even now struggles to be seen.

Terence Mervyn Rattigan was born on 10 June 1911, a wet Saturday a few days before George V's coronation. His father, Frank, was in the diplomatic corps and Terry's parents were often posted abroad, leaving him to be raised by his paternal grandmother. Frank Rattigan was a geographically and emotionally distant man, who pursued a string of little-disguised affairs throughout his marriage. Rattigan would later draw on these memories when he created Mark St Neots, the bourgeois Casanova of *Who is Sylvia?* Rattigan was much closer to his mother, Vera Rattigan, and they remained close friends until her death in 1971.

Rattigan's parents were not great theatregoers, but Frank Rattigan's brother had married a Gaiety Girl, causing a minor family uproar, and an apocryphal story suggests that the 'indulgent aunt' reported as taking the young Rattigan to the theatre may have been this scandalous relation.[2] And when, in the summer of 1922, his family went to stay in the country cottage of the drama critic Hubert Griffiths, Rattigan avidly worked through his extensive library of playscripts. Terry went to Harrow in 1925, and there maintained both his somewhat

illicit theatregoing habit and his insatiable reading, reputedly
devouring every play in the school library. Apart from
contemporary authors like Galsworthy, Shaw and Barrie, he also
read the plays of Chekhov, a writer whose crucial influence he
often acknowledged.[3]

His early attempts at writing, while giving little sign of his later
sophistication, do indicate his ability to absorb and reproduce
his own theatrical experiences. There was a ten-minute
melodrama about the Borgias entitled *The Parchment*, on the
cover of which the author recommends with admirable
conviction that a suitable cast for this work might comprise
'Godfrey Tearle, Gladys Cooper, Marie Tempest, Matheson
Lang, Isobel Elsom, Henry Ainley… [and] Noël Coward'.[4] At
Harrow, when one of his teachers demanded a French playlet
for a composition exercise, Rattigan, undaunted by his linguistic
shortcomings, produced a full-throated tragedy of deception,
passion and revenge which included the immortal curtain line:
'COMTESSE. (*Souffrant terriblement.*) Non! non! non! Ah non!
Mon Dieu, non!'[5] His teacher's now famous response was
'French execrable: theatre sense first class'.[6] A year later, aged
fifteen, he wrote *The Pure in Heart,* a rather more substantial
play showing a family being pulled apart by a son's crime and
the father's desire to maintain his reputation. Rattigan's
ambitions were plainly indicated on the title pages, each of
which announced the author to be 'the famous playwrite and
author T. M. Rattigan.'[7]

Frank Rattigan was less than keen on having a 'playwrite' for a
son and was greatly relieved when in 1930, paving the way for a
life as a diplomat, Rattigan gained a scholarship to read History
at Trinity, Oxford. But Rattigan's interests were entirely
elsewhere. A burgeoning political conscience that had led him
to oppose the compulsory Officer Training Corps parades at
Harrow saw him voice pacifist and socialist arguments at
college, even supporting the controversial Oxford Union motion
'This House will in no circumstances fight for its King and
Country' in February 1933. The rise of Hitler (which he briefly
saw close at hand when he spent some weeks in the Black
Forest in July 1933) and the outbreak of the Spanish Civil War
saw his radical leanings deepen and intensify. Rattigan never

lost his political compassion. After the war he drifted towards the Liberal Party, but he always insisted that he had never voted Conservative, despite the later conception of him as a Tory playwright of the establishment.[8]

Away from the troubled atmosphere of his family, Rattigan began to gain in confidence as the contours of his ambitions and his identity moved more sharply into focus. He soon took advantage of the university's theatrical facilities and traditions. He joined the Oxford Union Dramatic Society (OUDS), where contemporaries included Giles Playfair, George Devine, Peter Glenville, Angus Wilson and Frith Banbury. Each year, OUDS ran a one-act play competition and in Autumn 1931 Rattigan submitted one. Unusually, it seems that this was a highly experimental effort, somewhat like Konstantin's piece in *The Seagull*. George Devine, the OUDS president, apparently told the young author, 'Some of it is absolutely smashing, but it goes too far.'[9] Rattigan was instead to make his first mark as a somewhat scornful reviewer for the student newspaper, *Cherwell*, and as a performer in the Smokers (OUDS's private revue club), where he adopted the persona and dress of 'Lady Diana Coutigan', a drag performance which allowed him to discuss leading members of the Society with a barbed camp wit.[10]

That the name of his Smokers persona echoed the contemporary phrase, 'queer as a coot', indicates Rattigan's new-found confidence in his homosexuality. In February 1932, Rattigan played a tiny part in the OUDS production of *Romeo and Juliet*, which was directed by John Gielgud and starred Peggy Ashcroft and Edith Evans (women undergraduates were not admitted to OUDS, and professional actresses were often recruited). Rattigan's failure to deliver his one line correctly raised an increasingly embarrassing laugh every night (an episode which he reuses to great effect in *Harlequinade*). However, out of this production came a friendship with Gielgud and his partner, John Perry. Through them, Rattigan was introduced to theatrical and homosexual circles, where his youthful 'school captain' looks were much admired.

A growing confidence in his sexuality and in his writing led to his first major play. In 1931, he shared rooms with a contemporary of his, Philip Heimann, who was having an affair with Irina Basilevich, a mature student. Rattigan's own feelings for Heimann completed an eternal triangle that formed the basis of the play he co-wrote with Heimann, *First Episode*. This play was accepted for production in Surrey's 'Q' theatre; it was respectfully received and subsequently transferred to the Comedy Theatre in London's West End, though carefully shorn of its homosexual subplot. Despite receiving only £50 from this production (and having put £200 into it), Rattigan immediately dropped out of college to become a full-time writer.

Frank Rattigan was displeased by this move, but made a deal with his son. He would give him an allowance of £200 a year for two years and let him live at home to write; if at the end of that period, he had had no discernible success, he would enter a more secure and respectable profession. With this looming deadline, Rattigan wrote quickly. *Black Forest*, an O'Neill-inspired play based on his experiences in Germany in 1933, is one of the three that have survived. Rather unwillingly, he collaborated with Hector Bolitho on an adaptation of the latter's novel, *Grey Farm*, which received a disastrous New York production in 1940. Another project was an adaptation of *A Tale of Two Cities*, written with Gielgud; this fell through at the last minute when Donald Albery, the play's potential producer, received a complaint from actor-manager John Martin-Harvey who was beginning a farewell tour of his own adaptation, *The Only Way*, which he had been performing for forty-five years. As minor compensation, Albery invited Rattigan to send him any other new scripts. Rattigan sent him a play provisionally titled *Gone Away*, based on his experiences in a French-language summer school in 1931. Albery took out a nine-month option on it, but no production appeared.

By mid-1936, Rattigan was despairing. His father had secured him a job with Warner Brothers as an in-house screenwriter, which was reasonably paid; but Rattigan wanted success in the theatre, and his desk-bound life at Teddington Studios seemed unlikely to advance this ambition. By chance, one of Albery's productions was unexpectedly losing money, and the wisest course of action seemed to be to pull the show and replace it with something cheap. Since *Gone Away* required a relatively small cast and only one set, Albery quickly arranged for a production. Harold French, the play's director, had only one qualm: the title. Rattigan suggested *French Without Tears*, which was immediately adopted.

After an appalling dress rehearsal, no one anticipated the rapturous response of the first-night audience, led by Cicely Courtneidge's infectious laugh. The following morning Kay Hammond, the show's female lead, discovered Rattigan surrounded by the next day's reviews. 'But I don't believe it,' he said. 'Even *The Times* likes it.'[11]

French Without Tears played over 1000 performances in its three-year run and Rattigan was soon earning £100 a week. He moved out of his father's home, wriggled out of his Warner Brothers contract, and dedicated himself to spending the money as soon as it came in. Partly this was an attempt to defer the moment when he had to follow up this enormous success. In the event, both of his next plays were undermined by the outbreak of war.

After the Dance, an altogether more bleak indictment of the Bright Young Things' failure to engage with the iniquities and miseries of contemporary life, opened, in June 1939, to euphoric reviews; but only a month later the European crisis was darkening the national mood and audiences began to dwindle. The play was pulled in August after only sixty performances. *Follow My Leader* was a satirical farce closely based on the rise of Hitler, co-written with an Oxford contemporary, Tony Goldschmidt (writing as Anthony Maurice in case anyone thought he was German). It suffered an alternative fate. Banned from production in 1938, owing to the Foreign Office's belief that 'the production of this play at this time would not be in the best interests of the country',[12] it finally received its premiere in 1940, by which time Rattigan and Goldschmidt's mild satire failed to capture the real fears that the war was unleashing in the country.

Rattigan's insecurity about writing now deepened. An interest in Freud, dating back to his Harrow days, encouraged him to visit a psychiatrist that he had known while at Oxford, Dr Keith Newman. Newman exerted a Svengali-like influence on Rattigan and persuaded the pacifist playwright to join the RAF as a means of curing his writer's block. Oddly, this unorthodox treatment seemed to have some effect; by 1941, Rattigan was writing again. On one dramatic sea crossing, an engine failed, and with everyone forced to jettison all excess baggage and possessions, Rattigan threw the hard covers and blank pages from the notebook containing his new play, stuffing the precious manuscript into his jacket.

Rattigan drew on his RAF experiences to write a new play, *Flare Path*. Bronson Albery and Bill Linnit who had supported *French Without Tears* both turned the play down, believing that the last thing that the public wanted was a play about the war.[13] H. M. Tennent Ltd., led by the elegant Hugh 'Binkie' Beaumont, was the third management offered the script; and in 1942, *Flare Path* opened in London, eventually playing almost 700 performances. Meticulously interweaving the stories of three couples against the backdrop of wartime uncertainty, Rattigan found himself 'commended, if not exactly as a professional playwright, at least as a promising apprentice who had definitely begun to learn the rudiments of his job'.[14] Beaumont, already on the way to becoming the most powerful and successful West End producer of the era, was an influential ally for Rattigan. There is a curious side-story to this production; Dr Keith Newman decided to watch 250 performances of this play and write up the insights that his 'serial attendance' had afforded him. George Bernard Shaw remarked that such playgoing behaviour 'would have driven me mad; and I am not sure that [Newman] came out of it without a slight derangement'. Shaw's caution was wise.[15] In late 1945, Newman went insane and eventually died in a psychiatric hospital.

Meanwhile, Rattigan had achieved two more successes; the witty farce, *While the Sun Shines*, and the more serious, though politically clumsy, *Love in Idleness* (retitled *O Mistress Mine* in America). He had also co-written a number of successful films, including *The Day Will Dawn, Uncensored, The Way to the Stars* and an adaptation of *French Without Tears*. By the end of 1944, Rattigan had three plays running in the West End, a record only beaten by Somerset Maugham's four in 1908.

Love in Idleness was dedicated to Henry 'Chips' Channon, the Tory MP who had become Rattigan's lover. Channon's otherwise gossipy diaries record their meeting very discreetly:

'I dined with Juliet Duff in her little flat... also there, Sibyl
Colefax and Master Terence Rattigan, and we sparkled over the
Burgundy. I like Rattigan enormously, and feel a new friendship
has begun. He has a flat in Albany.'[16] Tom Driberg's rather less
discreet account fleshes out the story: Channon's 'seduction of
the playwright was almost like the wooing of Danaë by Zeus –
every day the playwright found, delivered to his door, a splendid
present – a case of champagne, a huge pot of caviar, a Cartier
cigarette box in two kinds of gold... In the end, of course, he
gave in, saying apologetically to his friends, "How can one
not?".'[17] It was a very different set in which Rattigan now
moved, one that was wealthy and conservative, the very people
he had criticised in *After the Dance*. Rattigan did not share the
complacency of many of his friends, and his next play revealed
a deepening complexity and ambition.

For a long time, Rattigan had nurtured a desire to become
respected as a serious writer; the commercial success of *French
Without Tears* had, however, sustained the public image of
Rattigan as a wealthy, young, light-comedy writer-about-town.[18]
With *The Winslow Boy*, which premiered in 1946, Rattigan
began to turn this image around. In doing so he entered a new
phase as a playwright. As one contemporary critic observed,
this play 'put him at once into the class of the serious and
distinguished writer'.[19] The play, based on the Archer-Shee case
in which a family attempted to sue the Admiralty for a false
accusation of theft against their son, featured some of Rattigan's
most elegantly crafted and subtle characterisation yet. The
famous second curtain, when the barrister Robert Morton
subjects Ronnie Winslow to a vicious interrogation before
announcing that 'The boy is plainly innocent. I accept the
brief', brought a joyous standing ovation on the first night. No
less impressive is the subtle handling of the concept of 'justice'
and 'rights' through the play of ironies which pits Morton's
liberal complacency against Catherine Winslow's feminist
convictions.

Two years later, Rattigan's *Playbill*, comprising the one-act
plays *The Browning Version* and *Harlequinade*, showed an ever
deepening talent. The latter is a witty satire of the kind of
touring theatre encouraged by the new Committee for the

Encouragement of Music and Arts (CEMA, the immediate forerunner of the Arts Council). But the former's depiction of a failed, repressed Classics teacher evinced an ability to choreograph emotional subtleties on stage that outstripped anything Rattigan had yet demonstrated.

Adventure Story, which in 1949 followed hard on the heels of *Playbill*, was less successful. An attempt to dramatise the emotional dilemmas of Alexander the Great, Rattigan seemed unable to escape the vernacular of his own circle, and the epic scheme of the play sat oddly with Alexander's more prosaic concerns.

Rattigan's response to both the critical bludgeoning of this play and the distinctly lukewarm reception of *Playbill* on Broadway was to write a somewhat extravagant article for the *New Statesman*. 'Concerning the Play of Ideas' was a desire to defend the place of 'character' against those who would insist on the pre-eminence in drama of ideas.[20] The essay is not clear and is couched in such teasing terms that it is at first difficult to see why it should have secured such a fervent response. James Bridie, Benn Levy, Peter Ustinov, Sean O'Casey, Ted Willis, Christopher Fry and finally George Bernard Shaw all weighed in to support or condemn the article. Finally Rattigan replied in slightly more moderate terms to these criticisms insisting (and the first essay reasonably supports this) that he was not calling for the end of ideas in the theatre, but rather for their inflection through character and situation.[21] However, the damage was done (as, two years later, with his 'Aunt Edna', it would again be done). Rattigan was increasingly being seen as the arch-proponent of commercial vacuity.[22]

The play Rattigan had running at the time added weight to his opponents' charge. Originally planned as a dark comedy, *Who is Sylvia?* became a rather more frivolous thing both in the writing and the playing. Rattled by the failure of *Adventure Story*, and superstitiously aware that the new play was opening at the Criterion, where fourteen years before *French Without Tears* had been so successful, Rattigan and everyone involved in the production had steered it towards light farce and obliterated the residual seriousness of the original conceit.

Rattigan had ended his affair with Henry Channon and taken up with Kenneth Morgan, a young actor who had appeared in *Follow My Leader* and the film of *French Without Tears*. However, the relationship had not lasted and Morgan had for a while been seeing someone else. Rattigan's distress was compounded one day in February 1949, when he received a message that Morgan had killed himself. Although horrified, Rattigan soon began to conceive an idea for a play. Initially it was to have concerned a homosexual relationship, but Beaumont, his producer, persuaded him to change the relationship to a heterosexual one.[23] At a time when the Lord Chamberlain refused to allow any plays to be staged that featured homosexuality, such a proposition would have been a commercial impossibility. The result is one of the finest examples of Rattigan's craft. The story of Hester Collyer, trapped in a relationship with a man incapable of returning her love, and her transition from attempted suicide to groping, uncertain self-determination is handled with extraordinary economy, precision and power. The depths of despair and desire that Rattigan plumbs have made *The Deep Blue Sea* one of his most popular and moving pieces.

1953 saw Rattigan's romantic comedy *The Sleeping Prince*, planned as a modest, if belated, contribution to the Coronation festivities. However, the project was hypertrophied by the insistent presence of Laurence Olivier and Vivien Leigh in the cast and the critics were disturbed to see such whimsy from the author of *The Deep Blue Sea*.

Two weeks after its opening, the first two volumes of Rattigan's *Collected Plays* were published. The preface to the second volume introduced one of Rattigan's best-known, and most notorious creations: Aunt Edna. 'Let us invent,' he writes, 'a character, a nice respectable, middle-class, middle-aged, maiden lady, with time on her hands and the money to help her pass it.'[24] Rattigan paints a picture of this eternal theatregoer, whose bewildered disdain for modernism ('Picasso – "those dreadful reds, my dear, and why three noses?"')[25] make up part of the particular challenge of dramatic writing. The intertwined commercial and cultural pressures that the audience brings with it exert considerable force on the playwright's work.

Rattigan's creation brought considerable scorn upon his head. But Rattigan is neither patronising nor genuflecting towards Aunt Edna. The whole essay is aimed at demonstrating the crucial role of the audience in the theatrical experience. Rattigan's own sense of theatre was *learned* as a member of the audience, and he refuses to distance himself from this woman: 'despite my already self-acknowledged creative ambitions I did not in the least feel myself a being apart. If my neighbours gasped with fear for the heroine when she was confronted with a fate worse than death, I gasped with them'.[26] But equally, he sees his job as a writer to engage in a gentle tug-of-war with the audience's expectations: 'although Aunt Edna must never be made mock of, or bored, or befuddled, she must equally not be wooed, or pandered to or cosseted'.[27] The complicated relation between satisfying and surprising this figure may seem contradictory, but as Rattigan notes, 'Aunt Edna herself is indeed a highly contradictory character.'[28]

But Rattigan's argument, as in the 'Play of Ideas' debate before it, was taken to imply an insipid pandering to the unchallenging expectations of his audience. Aunt Edna dogged his career from that moment on and she became such a byword for what theatre should *not* be that in 1960, the Questors Theatre, Ealing, could title a triple-bill of Absurdist plays, 'Not For Aunt Edna'.[29]

Rattigan's next play did help to restore his reputation as a serious dramatist. *Separate Tables* was another double-bill, set in a small Bournemouth hotel. The first play develops Rattigan's familiar themes of sexual longing and humiliation while the second pits a man found guilty of interfering with women in a local cinema against the self-appointed moral jurors in the hotel. The evening was highly acclaimed and the subsequent Broadway production a rare American success.

However, Rattigan's reign as the leading British playwright was about to be brought to an abrupt end. In a car from Stratford to London, early in 1956, Rattigan spent two and a half hours informing his Oxford contemporary George Devine why the new play he had discovered would not work in the theatre. When Devine persisted, Rattigan answered 'Then I know nothing about plays.' To which Devine replied, 'You know everything about plays, but you don't know a fucking thing about *Look Back in Anger.*'[30] Rattigan only barely attended the first night. He and Hugh Beaumont wanted to leave at the interval until the critic T. C. Worsley persuaded them to stay.[31]

The support for the English Stage Company's initiative was soon overwhelming. Osborne's play was acclaimed by the influential critics Kenneth Tynan and Harold Hobson, and the production was revived frequently at the Court, soon standing as the banner under which that disparate band of men (and women), the Angry Young Men, would assemble. Like many of his contemporaries, Rattigan decried the new movements, Beckett and Ionesco's turn from Naturalism, the wild invective of Osborne, the passionate socialism of Wesker, the increasing influence of Brecht. His opposition to them was perhaps intemperate, but he knew what was at stake: 'I may be prejudiced, but I'm pretty sure it won't survive,' he said in 1960, 'I'm prejudiced because if it *does* survive, I know I won't.'[32]

Such was the power and influence of the new movement that Rattigan almost immediately seemed old-fashioned. And from now on, his plays began to receive an almost automatic panning. His first play since *Separate Tables* (1954) was *Variation on a Theme* (1958). But between those dates the critical mood had changed. To make matters worse, there was the widely publicised story that nineteen-year-old Shelagh Delaney had written the successful *A Taste of Honey* in two weeks after having seen *Variation on a Theme* and deciding that she could do better. A more sinister aspect of the response was the increasingly open accusation that Rattigan was dishonestly concealing a covert homosexual play within an apparently heterosexual one. The two champions of Osborne's play, Tynan and Hobson, were joined by Gerard Fay in the *Manchester Guardian* and Alan Brien in the *Spectator* to ask 'Are Things What They Seem?'[33]

When he is not being attacked for smuggling furtively homosexual themes into apparently straight plays, Rattigan is also criticised for lacking the courage to 'come clean' about his sexuality, both in his life and in his writing.[34] But neither of these criticisms really hit the mark. On the one hand, it is rather disingenuous to suggest that Rattigan should have 'come out'. The 1950s were a difficult time for homosexual men. The flight to the Soviet Union of Burgess and Maclean in 1951 sparked off a major witch-hunt against homosexuals, especially those in prominent positions. Cecil Beaton and Benjamin Britten were rumoured to be targets.[35] The police greatly stepped up the investigation and entrapment of homosexuals and prosecutions rose dramatically at the end of the forties, reaching a peak in 1953–4. One of their most infamous arrests for importuning, in October 1953, was that of John Gielgud.[36]

But neither is it quite correct to imply that somehow Rattigan's plays are *really* homosexual. This would be to misunderstand the way that homosexuality figured in the forties and early fifties. Wartime London saw a considerable expansion in the number of pubs and bars where homosexual men (and women) could meet. This network sustained a highly sophisticated system of gestural and dress codes, words and phrases that could be used to indicate one's sexual desires, many of them drawn from theatrical slang. But the illegality of any homosexual activity ensured that these codes could never become *too* explicit, *too* clear. Homosexuality, then, was explored and experienced through a series of semi-hidden, semi-open codes of behaviour; the image of the iceberg, with the greater part of its bulk submerged beneath the surface, was frequently employed.[37] And this image is, of course, one of the metaphors often used to describe Rattigan's own playwriting.

Reaction came in the form of a widespread paranoia about the apparent increase in homosexuality. The fifties saw a major drive to seek out, understand, and often 'cure' homosexuality. The impetus of these investigations was to bring the unspeakable and underground activities of, famously, 'Evil Men' into the open, to make it fully visible. The Wolfenden Report of 1957 was, without doubt, a certain kind of liberalising document in its recommendation that consensual sex between adult men in private be legalised. However the other side of its effect is to reinstate the integrity of those boundaries – private/public, hidden/exposed, homosexual/heterosexual – which homosexuality was broaching. The criticisms of Rattigan are precisely part of this same desire to divide, clarify and expose.

Many of Rattigan's plays were originally written with explicit homosexual characters (*French Without Tears*, *The Deep Blue*

Sea and *Separate Tables*, for example), which he then changed.[38] But many more of them hint at homosexual experiences and activities: the relationship between Tony and David in *First Episode*, the Major in *Follow My Leader* who is blackmailed over an incident in Baghdad ('After all,' he explains, 'a chap's only human, and it was a deuced hot night – '),[39] the suspiciously polymorphous servicemen of *While the Sun Shines*, Alexander the Great and T. E. Lawrence from *Adventure Story* and *Ross*, Mr Miller in *The Deep Blue Sea* and several others. Furthermore, rumours of Rattigan's own bachelor life circulated fairly widely. As indicated above, Rattigan always placed great trust in the audiences of his plays, and it was the audience that had to decode and reinterpret these plays. His plays cannot be judged by the criterion of 'honesty' and 'explicitness' that obsessed a generation after Osborne. They are plays which negotiate sexual desire through structures of hint, implications and metaphor. As David Rudkin has suggested, 'the craftsmanship of which we hear so much loose talk seems to me to arise from deep psychological necessity, a drive to organise the energy that arises out of his own pain. Not to batten it down but to invest it with some expressive clarity that speaks immediately to people, yet keeps itself hidden.'[40]

The shifts in the dominant view of both homosexuality and the theatre that took place in the fifties account for the brutal decline of Rattigan's career. He continued writing, and while *Ross* (1960) was reasonably well received, his ill-judged musical adaptation of *French Without Tears*, *Joie de Vivre* (1960), was a complete disaster, not assisted by a liberal bout of laryngitis among the cast, and the unexpected insanity of the pianist.[41] It ran for four performances.

During the sixties, Rattigan was himself dogged with ill-health: pneumonia and hepatitis were followed by leukaemia. When his death conspicuously failed to transpire, this last diagnosis was admitted to be incorrect. Despite this, he continued to write, producing the successful television play *Heart to Heart* in 1962, and the stage play *Man and Boy* the following year, which received the same sniping that greeted *Variation on a Theme*. In 1964, he wrote *Nelson – a Portrait in Miniature* for Associated Television, as part of a short season of his plays.

It was at this point that Rattigan decided to leave Britain and live abroad. Partly this decision was taken for reasons of health; but partly Rattigan just seemed no longer to be welcome. Ironically, it was the same charge being levelled at Rattigan that he had faced in the thirties, when the newspapers thundered against the those who had supported the Oxford Union's pacifist motion as 'woolly-minded Communists, practical jokers and sexual indeterminates'.[42] As he confessed in an interview late in his life, 'Overnight almost, we were told we were old-fashioned and effete and corrupt and finished, and... I somehow accepted Tynan's verdict and went off to Hollywood to write film scripts.'[43] In 1967 he moved to Bermuda as a tax exile. A stage adaptation of his Nelson play, as *Bequest to the Nation*, had a lukewarm reception.

Rattigan had a bad sixties, but his seventies seemed to indicate a turnaround in his fortunes and reputation. At the end of 1970, a successful production of *The Winslow Boy* was the first of ten years of acclaimed revivals. In 1972, Hampstead Theatre revived *While the Sun Shines*, and a year later the Young Vic was praised for its *French Without Tears*. In 1976 and 1977 *The Browning Version* was revived at the King's Head and *Separate Tables* at the Apollo. Rattigan briefly returned to Britain in 1971, pulled partly by his renewed fortune and partly by the fact that he was given a knighthood in the New Year's honours list. Another double-bill followed in 1973: *In Praise of Love* comprised the weak *Before Dawn* and the moving tale of emotional concealment and creativity, *After Lydia*. Critical reception was more respectful than usual, although the throwaway farce of the first play detracted from the quality of the second.

Cause Célèbre, commissioned by BBC Radio and others, concerned the Rattenbury case, in which Alma Rattenbury's aged husband was beaten to death by her eighteen-year-old lover. Shortly after its radio premiere, Rattigan was diagnosed with bone cancer. Rattigan's response, having been through the false leukaemia scare in the early sixties, was to greet the news with unruffled elegance, welcoming the opportunity to 'work harder and indulge myself more'.[44] The hard work included a play about the Asquith family and a stage adaptation of *Cause Célèbre*, but, as production difficulties began to arise over the latter, the Asquith play slipped out of Rattigan's grasp. Although very ill, he returned to Britain, and on 4 July 1977, he was taken by limousine from his hospital bed to Her Majesty's Theatre, where he watched his last ever premiere. A fortnight later he had a car drive him around the West End where two of his plays were then running before boarding the plane for the last time. On 30 November 1977, in Bermuda, he died.

As Michael Billington's perceptive obituary noted, 'his whole work is a sustained assault on English middle-class values: fear of emotional commitment, terror in the face of passion, apprehension about sex'.[45] In death, Rattigan began once again to be seen as someone critically opposed to the values with which he had so long been associated, a writer dramatising dark moments of bleak compassion and aching desire.

Notes

1. Quoted in Rattigan's *Daily Telegraph* obituary (1 December 1977).

2. Michael Darlow and Gillian Hodson. *Terence Rattigan: The Man and His Work*. London and New York: Quartet Books, 1979, p. 26.

3. See, for example, Sheridan Morley. 'Terence Rattigan at 65.' *The Times*. (9 May 1977).

4. Terence Rattigan. Preface. *The Collected Plays of Terence Rattigan: Volume Two*. London: Hamish Hamilton, 1953, p. xv.

5. *Ibid.,* p. viii.

6. *Ibid.*, p. vii.

7. *Ibid.*, p. vii.

8. cf. Sheridan Morley, *op. cit.*

9. Humphrey Carpenter. *OUDS: A Centenary History of the Oxford University Dramatic Society*. With a Prologue by Robert Robinson. Oxford: Oxford University Press, 1985, p. 123.

10. Rattigan may well have reprised this later in life. John Osborne, in his autobiography, recalls a friend showing him a picture of Rattigan performing in an RAF drag show: 'He showed me a photograph of himself with Rattigan, dressed in a *tutu*, carrying a wand, accompanied by a line of aircraftsmen, during which Terry had sung his own show-stopper, 'I'm just about the oldest fairy in the business. I'm quite the oldest fairy that you've ever seen".' John Osborne. *A Better Class of Person: An Autobiography, Volume I 1929–1956*. London: Faber and Faber, 1981, p. 223.

11. Darlow and Hodson *op. cit.*, p. 83.

12. Norman Gwatkin. Letter to Gilbert Miller, 28 July 1938. in: *Follow My Leader*. Lord Chamberlain's Correspondence: LR 1938. [British Library].

13. Richard Huggett. *Binkie Beaumont: Eminence Grise of the West Theatre 1933–1973*. London: Hodder & Stoughton, 1989, p. 308.

14. Terence Rattigan. Preface. *The Collected Plays of Terence Rattigan: Volume One*. London: Hamish Hamilton, 1953, p. xiv.

15. George Bernard Shaw, in: Keith Newman. *Two Hundred and Fifty Times I Saw a Play: or, Authors, Actors and Audiences*. With the facsimile of a comment by Bernard Shaw. Oxford: Pelagos Press, 1944, p. 2.

16. Henry Channon. *Chips: The Diaries of Sir Henry Channon*. Edited by Robert Rhodes James. Harmondsworth: Penguin, 1974, p. 480. Entry for 29 September 1944.

17. Tom Driberg. *Ruling Passions*. London: Jonathan Cape, 1977, p. 186.

18. See, for example, Norman Hart. 'Introducing Terence Rattigan,' *Theatre World*. xxxi, 171. (April 1939). p. 180 or Ruth Jordan. 'Another Adventure Story,' *Woman's Journal*. (August 1949), pp. 31–32.

19. Audrey Williamson. *Theatre of Two Decades*. New York and London: Macmillan, 1951, p. 100.

20. Terence Rattigan. 'Concerning the Play of Ideas,' *New Statesman and Nation*. (4 March 1950), pp. 241–242.

21 Terence Rattigan. 'The Play of Ideas,' *New Statesman and Nation*. (13 May 1950), pp. 545–546. See also Susan Rusinko, 'Rattigan versus Shaw: The 'Drama of Ideas' Debate'. in: *Shaw: The Annual of Bernard Shaw Studies: Volume Two*. Edited by Stanley Weintraub. University Park, Penn: Pennsylvania State University Press, 1982. pp. 171–78.

22. John Elsom writes that Rattigan's plays 'represented establishment

writing'. *Post-War British Drama*. Revised Edition. London: Routledge, 1979, p. 33.

23. B. A. Young. *The Rattigan Version: Sir Terence Rattigan and the Theatre of Character*. Hamish Hamilton: London, 1986, pp. 102–103; and Darlow and Hodson, *op. cit*., p. 196, 204n.

24. Terence Rattigan. *Coll. Plays: Vol. Two. op. cit.*, pp. xi–xii.

25. *Ibid.*, p. xii.

26. *Ibid.*, p. xiv.

27. *Ibid.*, p. xvi.

28. *Ibid.*, p. xviii.

29. Opened on 17 September 1960. cf. *Plays and Players*. vii, 11 (November 1960).

30. Quoted in Irving Wardle. *The Theatres of George Devine*. London: Jonathan Cape, 1978, p. 180.

31. John Osborne. *Almost a Gentleman: An Autobiography, Volume II 1955–1966*. London: Faber and Faber, 1991, p. 20.

32. Robert Muller. 'Soul-Searching with Terence Rattigan.' *Daily Mail*. (30 April 1960).

33. The headline of Hobson's review in the *Sunday Times*, 11 May 1958.

34. See, for example, Nicholas de Jongh. *Not in Front of the Audience: Homosexuality on Stage*. London: Routledge, 1992, pp. 55–58.

35. Kathleen Tynan. *The Life of Kenneth Tynan*. Corrected Edition. London: Methuen, 1988, p. 118.

36. Cf. Jeffrey Weeks. *Coming Out: Homosexual Politics in Britain from the Nineteenth Century to the Present*. Revised and Updated Edition. London and New York: Quartet, 1990, p. 58; Peter Wildeblood. *Against the Law*. London: Weidenfeld and Nicolson, 1955, p. 46. The story of Gielgud's arrest may be found in Huggett, *op. cit.,* pp. 429–431. It was Gielgud's arrest which apparently inspired Rattigan to write the second part of *Separate Tables*, although again, thanks this time to the Lord Chamberlain, Rattigan had to change the Major's offence to a heterosexual one. See Darlow and Hodson, *op. cit.*, p. 228.

37. See, for example, Rodney Garland's novel about homosexual life in London, *The Heart in Exile*. London: W. H. Allen, 1953, p. 104.

38. See note 36; and also 'Rattigan Talks to John Simon,' *Theatre Arts*. 46 (April 1962), p. 24.

39. Terence Rattigan and Anthony Maurice. *Follow My Leader.* Typescript. Lord Chamberlain Play Collection: 1940/2. Box 2506. [British Library].

40. Quoted in Darlow and Hodson, *op. cit.,* p. 15.

41. B. A. Young, *op. cit.,* p. 162.

42. Quoted in Darlow and Hodson, *op. cit.,* p. 56.

43. Quoted in Sheridan Morley, *op. cit.*

44. Darlow and Hodson, *op. cit.,* p. 308.

45. *Guardian*. (2 December 1977).

Who is Sylvia?

In the decade from the mid-forties to the mid-fifties, Terence Rattigan wrote his four best-remembered dramas, *The Winslow Boy*, *The Browning Version*, *The Deep Blue Sea* and *Separate Tables*. In 1950, halfway through that period, he also wrote perhaps his least-remembered and certainly most misunderstood play, *Who is Sylvia?* It was, as I will show, a struggle at every stage: for its author, the author's agent, its potential cast, and its reviewers. The play has never had a major revival, did not make it to Broadway, and has tended to be regarded as an oddity and a failure. *Who is Sylvia?* is a curiosity in his career; but it's a dramaturgical experiment of considerable interest and delicacy, very much ahead of its time, and also one of Rattigan's most turbulently personal pieces of work.

1949 had been something of a misstep in the middle of Rattigan's golden period. His attempt to write a historical epic about Alexander the Great, *Adventure Story*, was poorly received and ran for only 108 performances, a poor showing compared to *The Browning Version*'s 245 and *The Winslow Boy*'s 476. The critics considered that Rattigan's focus on Alexander's psychology had failed to capture the great clash of ideas and civilisations in fourth-century Persia. Stung by these remarks, Rattigan wrote an article 'Considering the Play of Ideas', in which he claimed that plays could not be driven by ideas, only by character. It was an incautious performance, poorly expressed and petulant in tone. After a succession of ever more eminent interlocutors refuted his claims, Rattigan responded in milder and more sophisticated terms, but the damage – as with the 'Aunt Edna' saga three years later – was long-lasting; he seemed to be turning his back on ideas, politics, the idea that theatre might be a place for thought rather than mere entertainment.[1]

That year had also seen a convulsion in Rattigan's own life. Ten years before, during the filming of the screen version of *French Without Tears*, Rattigan had begun a brief affair with a young actor in the film, Kenneth Morgan. Towards the end of the war they met up again and resumed their relationship, now on a more serious basis. Rattigan had previously kept his lovers at arm's length, but Morgan was different; Terry asked the young man to move in with him and found his usual role was reversed – the more Rattigan's ardour increased, the more Morgan's cooled. By the summer of 1948, their relationship was sharply deteriorating; Morgan resented being marginalised and patronised as 'Terry's boy' by the playwright's friends, and repeatedly threatened to leave.[2] With Rattigan in the throes of preparations for his new play, Morgan met another actor and moved in with him.

Believing Morgan to be the love of his life and convinced he would return, Rattigan was devastated to be informed, just before the one of the final previews of *Adventure Story*, that Kenneth Morgan, rejected by his new lover, had taken his own life. Rattigan saw in this terrible episode the seed of a play (which, after many transformations, would become *The Deep Blue Sea*[3]), but knew he could only write it once the emotional shock had begun to fade. Nonetheless, his next play, *Who is Sylvia?*, is also haunted by secret desires, the inequality of passion, and the elusiveness of love.

Immediately after *Adventure Story* opened in March 1949, Rattigan took himself off to The Stag and Hounds in Binfield to begin writing. Later he would claim that his work was so misconceived he 'had to tear up about fifty pages and start again'.[4] In fact, he didn't tear them up and most of those pages have remained, unread and unrecognised, in his personal papers. More strikingly, at Binfield, the fundamental structure of the play as it would eventually be performed and published was fixed and hardly deviated from.[5]

The play goes through three main evolutions. Its first, incomplete, draft is called *The Search for May*, sketched out in March 1949. The second draft, retitled *Green After April*, was completed later that year. The third draft closely reworks the second, the changes being made in consultation with cast and director, and is called *Who is Sylvia?* The story remains fundamentally the same: a man, married and with a son, is drawn to women who resemble a childhood sweetheart. We see

him at three stages of life – 1917, 1929,[6] and 1950 –
conducting, or attempting to conduct, affairs with three near-
identical women: a shop girl, a flapper, and a model. At every
turn his seduction is foiled: in the first act, by the arrival of the
young woman's brother; in the second, by the arrival of his son;
and in the third, by the arrival of his wife, who explains that she
has known about Sylvia and his assignations all along. The
change of titles reflects the changing name of his fantasy image:
from May, to April, to Sylvia.[7]

Rattigan was a meticulous structural planner of plays. He
understood the shape of his plays through the choreography of
entrances and exits, revelations, and conversational patterns. In
the notes he wrote for the first draft, for example, this is how he
describes Act I:

1. Mark – Doris.

2. Mark telephone.

3. Mark – Doris.

4. Mark – Doris – Mrs Williams (interruption).

5. Mark – Doris – Ethel.

6. Mark – Doris – Ethel – Oscar.

7. Oscar to change. Mark – Doris – Ethel.

8. Oscar back. Ethel – Doris to kitchen, to wash up.

9. Mark – Oscar.

10. Girls back. Mark – Oscar.

11. Mark out to get taxi. Oscar – Doris – Ethel.

12. Doris to bed. Oscar's doing. Oscar – Ethel.

13. Mark back with taxi. Sends it away.

14. Oscar Doris out to Savoy.

15. Air raid. Mark out.[8]

There are adjustments to the precise order of events, but this
remains, through all the drafts, right up to the final version as
published here, the shape of the first act. But what is perhaps more

striking about this structural plan is what it does *not* contain: characterisation, tone, meaning, subtext, dialogue. Indeed, a hundred very different plays could be written to this outline.

And it is the treatment of the material that changes most sharply. All the evidence is that Rattigan set out to write a rather serious play: an exploration of promiscuity, the search for an ideal love, and the dynamics of emotional immaturity. Notably, at the same time that he's formulating his blast against the 'Play of Ideas' for the *New Statesman*, the notes-to-self that accompany the incomplete first draft articulate not just the play's story but its ideas:

> The story of a man who looked for an ideal love through the physical side and found it on the non-physical, unrecognised until then.

> Moral. Compromise with life. Don't look for love. Let love look for you.

> Against romantic love. The search for it may keep a man occupied and happy, but finding it may be a disaster.

> What do I want to say? Nothing very much. Ideal love doesn't exist. A satisfactory relationship is more likely to exist on the non-physical, rather than the physical plane, but a man finds it hard to compromise with his body, and a division of life into the physical and non-physical may be the happiest solution. What about the wife? She needs it too. I cheat there by making her a bit of a freak. If she divided her life in the same way there'd be sure to be a catastrophe.

> The bachelor character will show the dangers of promiscuity – not too tragically I hope. He should have compromised too, and married, or worked out a durable and un-ideal relationship with someone.

> *Compromise* is the keynote. Look for the ideal if you want to, but you'd better realise now that it doesn't exist.

> The fact that it does (in one case in a thousand) complicates the issue. The sensible gamblers bet on *égalités*. But that's not so much fun as betting *en plein*. The one shot in a thousand may come up. In the play it doesn't.

Was it worth it? The answer must be – yes, it was. The compromise is difficult and unromantic, but it it's [sic] worth more than the alternative – an unsuccessful amateur sculptor, tied for life to a 'May' who will later turn out not to be May at all. May doesn't exist anyway. That's the point of the play.[9]

There is very little like this document in Rattigan's archives; rarely did he explicate 'the point of the play' in as full and lucid a way as this. And, strikingly, these notes do not evidently describe a light comedy; they seem to be notes for a stark examination of male sexuality and the need to reconcile sex with love, desire with daily life. The draft fragments have comic moments, but they are also very frank about the reality of the situation in a way that later drafts would not be.

In the first draft, Doris (yet to be been renamed Daphne) is surprised that Mark is uncomfortable answering questions about his wife:

DORIS. My, you are touchy. It's a perfectly ordinary question to ask, isn't it?

MARK. No. I don't think it is.

DORIS. Well, I've been out with quite a lot of married gentlemen in my time, and they've never objected to being asked about their wives. In fact, it's usually the one subject they like to spread themselves on.

MARK. Well, I'm afraid that doesn't apply to me.

DORIS. Oh well. No offence, I'm sure.

She smiles in silence. MARK *drains a glass of champagne.*

MARK (*at length*). I'm sorry, Doris. You must forgive me. You see, this is my first essay in the extra-marital –

DORIS. Come again.

MARK. This is the first time, since I married seven years ago, that I've been out with any other woman but my wife.

DORIS. Just fancy.[10]

The dialogue is broadly realistic for the period and unflinchingly places the mechanics of adultery, Mark's awkwardness, and Doris's sexual experience front and centre.

While this made for great moral and emotional complexity, Rattigan was concerned that if the conversations and situations seemed too real they would make problems for the play that its tripartite structure could not resolve. As he explained to Rex Harrison, 'too many awkward and uncomfortable questions were raised which in light comedy can be gaily brushed aside; to wit, what happens to the discarded mistresses? The more considerable, as people, those ladies are, the more you will find the audience will worry about them when they are abandoned by Mark.'[11]

So he started again, now pitching the play at a level of deliberate unreality. The play became lighter in tone, tripping gaily over the details of the affairs and remaining witty and lightly farcical. But it would be a mistake to assume that Rattigan wanted to shy away from the seriousness of his theme: his remarks to Rex Harrison make clear that his main concern was that the balance of the play would be disturbed with the audience caring less about Mark than his discarded girlfriends. And maintaining a balance of sympathies in the play gets to the heart of why this play was so important to Rattigan.

Rattigan told one interviewer that the play was 'based on the lives of two real people. A married couple... very good friends of mine.'[12] He was being coy because the married couple he had in mind were his own parents. Frank Rattigan married Vera Houston in 1905 but was a faithless husband. He would often visit Rattigan at school with a new young woman on his arm, 'improbable young ladies, who typically came from dress shops and had names like Cora,' says Rattigan's biographer, with an unconscious nod to *Who is Sylvia*? Once, when father and son went on holiday together, Terry was surprised to discover from the hotel register that he'd acquired a 'sister', the cover for Rattigan Senior's latest dalliance. Vera put up with all this, though it caused her great suffering, which she confided in her son.

Rattigan was by turns embarrassed for his father and angry on behalf of his mother, and had long wanted to write a play about

'The Major'.[13] There is no doubt that Mark is a portrait of
Frank. In the early notes for the play, Rattigan writes Mark's
Who's Who entry:

> *Mark Arbour* Who's Who. b. 1885. Eldest son of Sir John
> Arbour and Lucy, née Wackett. Education. Eton and abroad.
> Entered diplomatic service 1908, passing third Attaché 1908,
> 3rd Secretary 1911, 2nd Secretary 1915, 1st Secretary 1921,
> Counsellor of Embassy 1928, Chargé d'Affaires Athens
> 1929, Head of Near Eastern department Foreign Office 1930,
> Minister in Montevideo 1935, Minister in Belgrade 1938,
> Foreign Office 1939-45 (Accompanying P.M. to Yalta and
> Potsdam). Ambassador Warsaw 1945. Ambassador to Paris
> 1946. C.M.G. 1919. K.C.M G. 1936, created Lord Binfield
> 1946. M. 1909, Mary, 2nd daughter of Duke of Kelvedon,
> son (Peter) 1910, daughter (Elizabeth) 1911. Recreations:
> golf and sculpting.[14]

Here's the same entry, but I've replaced Mark's information
with Frank's:

> William Frank Arthur Rattigan. b. 1879. 2nd son of Sir
> William Henry Rattigan and Evelyn, née Higgins. Education.
> Harrow and Magdalen College, Oxford. Entered diplomatic
> service as attaché 1902, 3rd Secretary 1905, 2nd Secretary
> 1909, 1st Secretary 1916, Chargé d'Affaires Romania 1919,
> Counsellor of Embassy 1920. C.M.G. 1921. M. Vera,
> daughter of Arthur Houston K.C., son (Brian) 1908,
> (Terence) 1911. Recreations: philandering.

The first half of Mark's career almost exactly duplicates
Frank's, but six years later. The reason Frank's entry is much
shorter than Mark's is that Frank's career in diplomacy was cut
short by an undiplomatic incident in Constantinople, when he
was No. 2 in the British Embassy; in 1921, with Kemal
Atatürk's military campaign for Turkish nationhood growing
ever stronger, he told the Turkish Foreign Minister that Britain
would never agree to independence. Lord Curzon, the foreign
secretary, was furious at having the Government's hands tied in
this fashion, and Frank was quietly pensioned off.[15]

A deep ambivalence towards Mark's affairs runs through the
play. Rattigan's two biographers are divided over his intentions:

for Wansell, *Who is Sylvia?* is an 'attempt to explain his father to his mother, providing the woman he cared about so deeply with something approaching a reasoned explanation for her husband's behaviour'; for Darlow, 'Rattigan intended to put his father on the stage and damn him'.[16] It's clear from Rattigan's original notes that he was unsure what attitude to take towards his principal character's behaviour; writing, in visible confusion: 'Of course one will sympathise with it – if one doesn't it's a bad play – but I suppose we can two-facedly deplore it at the same time. (No.)'[17] He must have had mixed feelings about his father in any case; although he deplored the pain Frank was causing Vera, he occasionally played Oscar to Frank's Mark, letting his father use his own flat for assignations.[18]

But there's a further reason for the ambivalence in the play. In some ways, Mark is also a portrait of Rattigan himself. Oscar describes Mark in the first act as an 'emotional Peter Pan', someone who 'refuses to come out of the emotional nursery'. Mark rejoins: 'what's wrong with that? I prefer to keep my emotions adolescent. They're far more enjoyable than adult ones' (p. 35). In the 1940s and 1950s, one of the most influential accounts of homosexuality was drawn from Freudian psychoanalysis, and explained it as a kind of arrested development; children, so the argument goes, will have all kinds of desires and objects as infants but 'normally' most of these will be discarded during the Oedipal Phase leaving only heterosexual object-choices. To still have erotic attachments to people of your own sex is to have failed to get through the Oedipal Phase 'correctly'. The British Medical Association in *Homosexuality and Prostitution*, for example, concludes that to be an adult homosexual 'represents some immaturity of development'. Eustace Chesser in *Odd Man Out: Homosexuality in Men and Women* puts it more bluntly: 'the invert has not grown up'.[19]

Implausible though these accounts seem to us now, they were popular in the mid-century, and Rattigan, an avid reader of Freud since school, held to their explanation of his own sexual feelings. Furthermore, he understood very well the requirement to lead something of a double life, just as Mark does. The fear of exposure, which runs right through the play, is not merely the

traditional tension of a bedroom farce, but was a real daily
concern for Rattigan. In *The Man Who Loved Redheads*,
Rattigan's screen adaptation of *Who is Sylvia?*, we see Mark
and Sylvia's first encounter as young teenagers, in a cupboard,
playing hide-and-seek. No sooner have they shared a first,
furtive kiss than the doors are flung open and 'light shines in on
the guilty pair. A crowd of grinning and malevolent juvenile
faces appear in the doorway, and a chorus of catcalls and hoots
greet MARK and SYLVIA.'[20] It's an image direct from
Rattigan's deepest fears, mixing secret sexuality and invasive
public judgement.[21]

Further clues link Mark and Terry. There's a suggestion that
Mark is undecided between his career as a diplomat and his
desire to pursue sculpture, for which he has a gift. Rattigan
had a similar dilemma between diplomacy and creativity:
Frank wanted him to follow him into the Service, and it was
only the success of *French Without Tears* that prevented it.
Finally, we hear that soon after Mark's fleeting encounter with
the original Sylvia, she married and moved to South Africa.
One of Rattigan's first (unrequited) loves, Philip Heimann,
with whom he wrote *First Episode*, also married shortly after
they met and moved to South Africa; he may be Rattigan's
own great lost love.

All of which suggests that Mark is an image of two Rattigans,
père et fils; hence the ambivalence in the play. On one hand,
Rattigan, certainly in the final act, mocks the aged roués and
their hapless chasing after young women; on the other, he offers
a sympathetic portrait of a man pursuing a love of which society
would not approve. According to Michael Darlow, 'from these
conflicting intentions, the essential weaknesses of *Who is Sylvia?*
grew.'[22] The play was performed as a feather-light comedy, and
so it is usually disregarded as such. The moral dilemmas that
arise unbidden in the first draft have disappeared; indeed, for a
sex farce, it is remarkably chaste – the structure of each act is a
kind of *coitus interruptus* – and, as Doris remarks in Act Three,
the offstage bedroom is 'really never used' (p. 84).[23]

But while it is true that the play becomes lighter in the
rewriting, the move is not away from seriousness, but from
realism. The first signal of this is the indication that the three

young women to whom Mark is attracted are all played by the same actress. It gives the action of the play a hallucinatory quality that allows us access to Mark's subjectivity, invites us to share in his view of the world. Glen Byam Shaw, who Rattigan had asked to consider directing the play, declined the offer, and his reasons for doing so are telling: 'I should tend to give it a reality which you have so cleverly realised in the writing would be wrong. When you pointed out to me your reason for having the three parts played by one girl it said to me what I had tried to say to you but not been able to explain in definite terms.'[24]

The structure of the play is unusual in its rather formal triptych. We are given three snapshots of Mark's life and we are, for the most part, required to infer what has taken place between the acts. Some of the play's first critics found the play's structure rather repetitive, but with hindsight, after the similar and deliberate repetitions of plays like *Waiting for Godot* and *Look Back in Anger*, this may be one of the play's principal points of interest. It conveys both the obsessiveness of Mark's behaviour and also its pointlessness. His unconscious feelings generate a kind of stammering repetition of the original desire. In addition, the play's time-jumps mark it out as ahead of its time. There had been plays that leapt vigorously across the decades – J.B. Priestley's *Time and the Conways* (1937) or George Bernard Shaw's *Back to Methusaleh* (1922), for example – but the device was far less common than it is now. The separate periods emphasise the isolation of each act and, through the vivid recreation of each era's slang and cultural references, adds a sense of sparkling artifice that further takes us into Mark's head.[25]

Rattigan finished the second draft of his play in January 1950 and sent it to 'Binkie' Beaumont of H.M. Tennent, who had produced several of his comedies before, and also to his agent of almost twenty years, A.D. Peters. Beaumont was enthusiastic about the play and immediately began to put together the production team. To direct, they approached Anthony Quayle, best known for his work with the Shakespeare Memorial Theatre (later to become the Royal Shakespeare Company), another sign that Rattigan saw this fundamentally as a serious comedy.

Peters met Terry to discuss the play and was less than enthusiastic. Indeed, his criticisms were so fundamental that there seemed to be little of the play that was salvageable. When Rattigan tried to defend it, Peters is thought to have remarked rather drily that he thought it would be an 'extremely interesting first night', with the implication that his criticisms of the play would be vindicated. This enraged Rattigan, who wrote to him a couple of days later and sacked him as his agent for this play. He did so with immaculate politeness: 'Your criticisms were welcome – as all considered criticisms are at this stage – and their forthrightness is appreciated, but if I were to act on them I would, it seems to me, either have to rewrite the play entirely with a new construction or, let's face it, tear it up and forget about it.'[26] Instead, he would let his US agent, Harold Freedman, represent the play in both the UK and the US. Peters was horrified – 'Your letter gave me one of the biggest shocks I have ever had' – and begged him to reconsider, insisting that, as an agent, he felt he had a duty to offer constructive criticism, awkward though that may be: 'It is always a difficult and painful thing to criticise an author's work adversely,' he explained. 'It is like telling a mother that her newborn baby squints.'[27] Rattigan was unmoved, replying that 'you have left me in no doubt whatever that you have no basic faith in the play as it stood', and drew particular attention to his comment about the first-night audience, 'hardly a remark calculated to imbue an author – nervous at the best of times – with great confidence.'[28] This was the beginning of the end for their professional relationship. Rattigan would continue to work closely with Freedman and eventually abandoned A.D. Peters for Jan Van Loewen's agency instead.

Was it just this casual and thoughtless remark that caused the rift? It seems unlikely. As Peters bitterly – but rightly – remarked in a later letter to Terry, 'if your views are carried to their logical conclusion, agents will become mere yes-men, and every manuscript they receive will be a flawless masterpiece. Perhaps that is what agents ought to be. It would certainly make life easier for them.'[29] Rattigan could be thin-skinned but, even by his standards, this would have been a considerable overreaction. In fact, as he explained in a letter to Harold Freedman, he had reason to doubt Peters' professionalism. Another of his clients was J.B. Priestley, and the producer

Stephen Phillips had been considering a new comedy by him. When he came to discuss the production with the agent, Peters had reputedly said the play was 'one of the worst plays Priestley had ever written and "was embarrassingly unfunny".' Word of this had come to Rattigan, who concluded that Peters 'would be entirely unable to conceal his true opinion of [*Who is Sylvia?*] professionally, even if he tried – which, in view of Stephen's story – seems unlikely.' In addition, Rattigan insisted, his smug prediction of a frosty first night was 'unforgivable': 'He intended, apparently, to wait happily and complacently with folded arms for the audience's verdict which, if favourable, would make him money, and, if unfavourable, would give him a splendid chance of saying "I told you so". Binkie and I and the rest of us have all the work, heartache and worries. Peters collects the plums. Over my dead body.'[30]

Harold Freedman, in fact, was not without criticisms of the play himself. In a lengthy letter to Rattigan, he urged the playwright to rewrite the play, making it more serious: 'I am just wondering whether or not that in getting away from the heavy treatment you told me you had started the play out with, you have finally landed on too light a treatment for it.' He felt in particular that the Sylvia theme should be emphasised more strongly and argued that for Mark's wife Caroline to reveal she has known about Sylvia all along lets Mark off the hook of having to face up to his emotional immaturity.[31] Of course, Rattigan had already attempted to write this more serious play and did not want to go back to it, but promised to emphasise Sylvia's will-o'-the-wisp presence in the play and give Mark a more active role in the denouement.

Behind Freedman's remarks stood the figure of Rex Harrison. Mark St Neots is a difficult role, requiring an actor charismatic enough to seduce the audience from their moral doubts, quick-witted enough to play the comedy, and sophisticated enough to find the complexity in this man's failed thirty-three-year journey to recover his lost love. To author, agent and producer, Rex Harrison was the perfect choice. A suave, attractive, magnetic figure, he was both a leading man and excellent comic actor; his first big break was, in fact, in the first production of *French Without Tears*. In playing Mark he would also have had the advantage of being able to draw on his own considerable experience as an impenitent philanderer. Freedman's suggestions about the conclusion derived from Rex's view that 'when you get to the end of the play all he had to do was groan at Caroline's pointing this out to him and that out to him.'[32]

Rex Harrison repeated these concerns in a long letter to Rattigan a week later. His criticisms are threefold: he is unhappy that Caroline gets the best of the last act; he is also anxious that Denis gets the best of the second; and finally, he expresses some anxiety that Mark would fall for 'these giggly girls'. For a 'cultured, witty, man of the world' to fall in love with a 'silly, very common shop girl […] gold-digging Nora [and] mannequin and Mum's best friend Doris' risked making him look 'foolish'.[33]

Fairly obviously, these criticisms are a mixture of snobbery and actor's vanity, Harrison not wanting to compromise his suave star persona, nor to be upstaged by his co-stars. But he was a big star and his presence would guarantee a Broadway run of the play, so Rattigan responded at considerable length, setting out 'the ideas I had intended to underlie the play' so that they could both judge whether the ideas are wrong or the play has not brought them out sufficiently. As a result, we have a second substantial exposition of Rattigan's thinking on *Who is Sylvia?*

He begins by explaining that Sylvia is a fantasy and diagnoses Mark as:

> a fairly straightforward Oedipus subject in love with the mother image which he neatly divides into two halves, the upper half being represented by his wife and the lower half by his successive Sylvias. His conscious mind is acutely aware of the fact that the lower half of this image must never dominate the upper and he arranges his life accordingly.

In other words, his erotic life is sharply divided and 'it is to safeguard his marital life that he takes on extra-marital relationships'. And since he is trying not to harm his marriage but – on some level, anyway – to protect it, 'he *deliberately* chooses his extra-marital relationships from among those girls who could never menace his relationship with Caroline.' And this allows him, for most of the play, to have the best of both

worlds. 'Mark has a wife and son who he adores and who adore
him and a long series of pleasant, if rather vague, romantic
memories. He has had his cake and eaten it. Oscar has only had
his cake and at the end of his life is feeling very hungry – poor
old man.' He admits that 'this is the basis of a far more serious
play than I have written', but emphasises that it is not intended
to be a frivolous play but more of a fantasy. Referring to the
idea of having one actress play the three 'Sylvias', he notes that
'it introduces the note of fantasy which, I think, will be vastly
important to the play and will, also I am sure, give an audience
a very good clue to the secret of Mark's psychology'. As for
Rex's worries about being upstaged by his son and wife, he tries
to be reassuring: 'the comedy, I am sure, consists in his
discomfiture – you know how sadistic audiences are – and in his
enforced abandonment of paternal dignity.'[34] Again, the picture
Rattigan paints of his play is of a serious piece of work.

Rattigan's wooing of Rex Harrison was not ultimately
successful. In his first letter, Harold Freedman admitted to
doubts that Rex would take the part and a few days later cabled
to warn that Harrison was being talked about in connection with
a musical adaptation of *Anna and the King of Siam*, the film in
which Rex Harrison had starred in 1946.[35] He recommended
approaching other actors, but Rattigan was reluctant: he knew
Rex would be right for the part and would certainly be affronted
to know that other actors were being talked to about the role.
Rex, for his part, cabled in early March to confirm his interest.
Rattigan clumsily attempted to turn this into a firm
commitment, a trap from which Rex nimbly escaped, explaining
that he only meant he'd tell Terry if he decided to take on
something else. He nonetheless insisted that he wanted to do the
part and begged Rattigan to keep the part for him. 'Will bear
with you till kingdom come,' cabled Rattigan in reply, 'or more
specifically about middle April.' These hopes were dashed at the
end of the month, when Harrison's wife, Lilli Palmer, was cast
in John Van Druten's *Bell, Book and Candle* in the autumn,
when Harrison would have had to be away playing Mark St
Neots, and so he turned the part down.[36]

Casting the lead role continued to elude the production team.
Rattigan was keen on Michael Wilding, who had been a big

success in *While the Sun Shines* but was now a big star in British films and regretfully had to turn the part down, returning, by post, 'your beautiful play & some pieces of my broken heart'.[37] David Niven was unavailable and John Mills also declined ('I have always wanted to do a play of yours and I absolutely hate having to say that I don't think this one is quite my cup of tea').[38] Michael Redgrave was apparently 'madly keen'[39] to play it, but his career in films was taking off and negotiating his time would have meant more delays. Robert Flemyng, on the other hand, was interested and his dates worked out. But Rattigan hesitated for five days. Why the delay? Rattigan knew Flemyng well; he was another alumnus of the first *French Without Tears* cast, but was he perhaps too light? Was he charismatic enough? Having been searching for his Mark since late January, however, Rattigan was getting concerned that the part could ever be cast and so cabled his old friend to offer him the role.

In the event, Bobby Flemyng had spoken to his old castmate, Rex Harrison, and shared his views of some of the play's shortcomings. Although he was less concerned about being upstaged by Caroline and Denis, he, too, felt that Mark needed to have more sophisticated tastes in women:

> We must see a little more of the man who is capable of being an ambassador – and what is more a brilliant one in one of the key appointments. You see it's only too easy for the soldier type, who is brilliant, and spends his spare time successfully fucking without any amorous entanglements – I knew quite a few in me [sic] time in the service. *But* Mark is quite another cup of tea.

Conspiratorially, he added:

> We don't have to tell each other, dear, that for numbers of our intelligence deception in the matter of romance is always disaster – in other words that we soon know when a lovely face is a bore, and *not* the romance we were rather hoping it would be.[40]

Rattigan's reply is not recorded but, in any event, he did not adjust his Sylvias.

With the lead actor in place, it became easier to start casting the
other roles. For the brief role of Caroline, they asked the
greatest stage comedienne of the day, Athene Seyler, who
responded with enthusiasm: 'this is brilliant stuff real high
comedy I'd love to do that charming five minutes.'[41] Esmond
Knight – after cavilling at the size of the role – agreed to play
Williams.[42] Roland Culver – yet another member of the first
French Without Tears cast – was hired to play Oscar. Indeed,
French Without Tears cast a long shadow over *Who is Sylvia?*,
not least after the decision was made to produce the show in the
Criterion Theatre, where the earlier play had been such a
success. Rattigan thought this a good idea, cabling that it
offered a 'small gross but excellent atmosphere and tradition for
light comedy thus obviating necessity excusing lightness of play
pre-production publicity'.[43] And when Mark explains that his
son has been 'at this place in Tours for three months and he
can't even write a line of a letter in reasonably correct French.
Keeps complaining that the daughter of the house has fallen in
love with him' (p. 51), he is neatly recapitulating the plot of
French Without Tears, an echo that would have been amplified
in the Criterion's auditorium.

The decision to play the Criterion seems to be part of a shift in
Rattigan's attitude, no longer defending the elements of
emotional fantasy in his play, instead capitulating to those
around him who preferred to see *Who is Sylvia?* as a light
comedy. This is how the theatre programme billed the play and
Rattigan himself told a journalist on the eve of its London
opening, 'This tonight is only a little comedy – light,
unemotional. Frankly, I planned it as a serious play. It just
turned into a frivolity.'[44]

The play had a short pre-London tour, opening at the
Cambridge Arts Theatre, moving to Brighton, and thence to
London. The production was not happy. Rattigan had
complained to some friends that Robert Flemyng was playing it
too ponderously – his friend Juliet Duff wrote to suggest that
'if poor Mr F. persists in playing it like Ibsen [, Noël Coward]
would be superb in the part, and give it just the careless gaiety
that it needs'[45] – but cabled Harold Freedman after press night
to blame 'Flemyng's inability to bring out the various

relationships in the play notably with Oscar thus making their
scenes together more like backchat between comedians than
conversation between very close friends'.[46] Flemyng,
meanwhile, was unhappy about the performance of Diane Hart,
playing all the Sylvias, and wrote to Rattigan that he was
privately re-rehearsing her and wanted Terry to drop in to
watch Tony Quayle redirect the first scene.[47] Rattigan's
secretary, Mary Herring, watched the dress rehearsal and
reported, 'It was dreadful, they were all as flat as pancakes.'
Terry toyed with bringing in Nigel Patrick as a last-minute
replacement for Flemyng.[48]

Regional critics were sometimes positive, the reviewer in the
Cambridge Daily News praising 'the great art of this superb
dramatist wedded to some of the most polished acting ever seen
on a stage long famous for outstanding performances'.[49] The
dominant tone is confusion; some found the play too long,
others too light. These confusions deepened when the play
opened in London. If the reviewers saw it as a light comedy,
they found it neither light nor comic enough. If they believed it
to be a serious play, they lamented that the play was
insufficiently serious. Speaking up for the latter tendency, *The
Times* declared that 'the first act is scattered with what seem to
be the bits and pieces of a serious intention' but wishes 'this
theme were treated seriously'.[50] Meanwhile, the headline of
Cecil Wilson's review in the *Daily Mail* summarised the former
view: 'Too Many Titters, Not Enough Laughs'. It is clear that
the critics did not know what to make of this play, which did not
fit into any known genre. Beverly Baxter makes this clear in the
Evening Standard: 'If we are to have sin, and there is a place for
sin in the theatre, it should be either tragic or amusing. Mr
Rattigan's sinners are neither.'[51]

Most perceptive was Alan Dent's review which noted, as no
other critic seemed to, that it is the combination of melancholy
and laughter that is distinctive and original about the play:

> Terence Rattigan's new play calls itself 'A light comedy' in
> the programme. Yet it is continuously concerned with that
> bitterest thing in life's comedy, the loss of illusion with the
> approach of age [...] Mr Rattigan's touch stays remarkably
> light, though his subject is here and there genuinely and

intractably serious and not really the stuff of frivolous
comedy [...] This is a comedy which keeps us sadly smiling
most of the time rather than in continuous laughter.[52]

Neither for the first nor last time, the critics would not allow
Rattigan to innovate, preferring to see him as a conventional
writer, working in conventional dramatic forms.

Rattigan was confident that 'normal audiences' would be less
flustered by *Who is Sylvia?*'s playfulness with tone and genre,
and consoled himself that the 'box-office is quite active'.[53]
Indeed, a little over two months later, critic Harold Hobson
reported to the *Christian Science Monitor* that '*Who is Sylvia?*
is one of the big successes of the current season. The critics
didn't like it and are considerably exasperated to find that the
public which is crowding the Criterion Theatre at every
performance, isn't paying any attention to their opinion.'[54] The
play eventually ran for almost a year, notching up a highly
respectable 381 performances. Rattigan did not benefit directly,
having agreed to waive his royalty in order to keep this very
personal play running.

There was talk of a film adaptation before *Who is Sylvia?* had
made its stage debut. Cary Grant was said to be interested in
playing Mark, with Carol Reed (most famous for *The Third
Man* in 1949) directing.[55] When the film finally appeared, it was
refashioned around the attributes of its female star, Moira
Shearer: the second-act Nora is transformed into Olga, a
Russian ballerina, giving Shearer a chance to showcase her
former career as a ballet dancer, while the play is retitled *The
Man Who Loved Redheads* to correspond to Shearer's Titian
curls. The play is opened up, as was customary, with its most
interesting innovation being a rather eccentric narrator, voiced
by Kenneth More, who barely seems on top of the story. When
the film opened in January 1955, one reviewer praised it as 'one
of the best British comedies for some time. A laughter-maker
that cannot fail to do excellent box-office business.'[56]

The play was performed (as *Vem är Sylvia?*), at the Vasateatern
with Håkan Westergren in the lead, in September 1951, to
considerable acclaim; and, some time later, at the Olimpia
Theatre, in Milan, under the title *Sylvia*, directed by Ernesto

Calindri, who also took the role of Oscar, with celebrated actor
Franco Volpi in the leading role. Then, apart from a scattering of
amateur productions, the play was almost entirely neglected, out
of print for over fifty years.

With hindsight, we can see *Who is Sylvia?* as a rather different
thing from the 'frivolity' that opened uncertainly onto the
Criterion stage in October 1950. It has some moments of terrific
comedy – Oscar's arrival in Act One, Denis's in Act Two, and
Mark's protests against Caroline in Act Three, for example – but
it also has what Michael Darlow calls 'a sense of something
darker lurking beneath the surface'.[57]

What was the lurking darkness? In some ways, Rattigan was
trying to come to terms with his father's faithless behaviour,
though Frank did not get to see himself affectionately guyed on
the Criterion stage. In July 1949, as his son was writing the
play, he suffered a stroke; in September 1950, with the play in
late rehearsal, he broke his leg and, despite hospital treatment,
was clearly in decline. He died eighteen months later. But also,
Rattigan is placing himself before the theatre's examining gaze.
His search for love, his promiscuity, the need for secrecy, all are
dramatised here, comically and sympathetically. And, in a kind
of living re-enactment of Mark's final epiphany, in the autumn
in which *Who is Sylvia?* opened, after twenty years of casual,
short-lived relationships, Rattigan met Michael Franklin, a
young man who became his lover, and would become a constant
companion for the rest of his life.

The stakes for *Who is Sylvia?* were very high. Despite its
unevenness, it remains one of Rattigan's most experimental and
unsettling plays. It is the work of a mature playwright asking
himself how to live and how to love.

Duologue

If *Who is Sylvia?* represents Rattigan coming to terms with his
father's life, *Duologue* is about his mother's. The play began life
as a piece for television, in a series called *A Touch of Venus*
(subtitled: 'Women Alone'), that comprised short monologues
for women written by established playwrights: amongst the

other authors in the series were J.B. Priestley, Emlyn Wiliams, and Frank Marcus. Rattigan wrote *All On Her Own* for one of his favourite actresses, Margaret Leighton, and it was broadcast on BBC2 in September 1968.

Rosemary is a widow who returns from a party and, a little drunkenly, starts addressing her dead husband. Through her reflections and recriminations, she comes to a sad realisation about their relationship, her behaviour, and the nature of his death. Margaret Leighton, immaculately coiffured, enormously elegant, her face just occasionally cracking to show fear, loneliness, misery, gives a very effective performance. The character's drunkenness gives her voice an insubstantial fluency, a sing-song quality, which manages to give a haunting quality to the naturalism of her performance. And despite the theatrical conventions of television production of the time, Leighton's performance is very televisual, low-key, detailed and subtle.[58] The monologue feels like a forerunner to a series like Alan Bennett's *Talking Heads* twenty years later.

Unusually for a television play, *All On Her Own* was published, in an American collection of *Best Short Plays of 1970*.[59] In 1974, a copy came into the hands of Alan and Maria Riccio Bryce, who had just started a small lunchtime fringe theatre in Kingston, opposite the railway station, called the Overground Theatre. They were looking for short plays and Maria had some experience acting in a New York university workshop production of *Separate Tables*, and she decided to direct a production. Margaret Stallard was engaged to play Rosemary. The Overground was very small, seating no more than thirty, and the play ran for just under a week, and played to an audience of 111.[60]

This was a far cry from the huge West End successes of Rattigan's golden era, but it was also a sign of a new generation, schooled in fringe theatre in rooms above pubs rather than glamorous openings on Shaftesbury Avenue. Two years later, in January 1976, Rattigan's revival got a significant boost when the King's Head, another fringe theatre, revived *The Browning Version*. Originally, Rattigan's one-act play was paired with *Carol's Christmas* by Frank Marcus, but the success of *The Browning Version* led to talk of a possible transfer. Rattigan told the *Sunday Times*, 'they wanted a curtain raiser. So I've redone this TV thing. It's about a woman in Hampstead reminiscing about her dead husband and gradually she begins to voice his thoughts as well as her own.' It was also an opportunity to find a stronger name for the play: 'Normally I'm secretive about titles but I'll tell you this one. I'm calling it *Duologue*. I'm rather pleased with that.'[61] He took the opportunity to reinstate some of the cuts he had made for the television programme and gave his heroine a last name, Hodge.[62] This final version of the script has never been published until now.

It displays many of Rattigan's great merits as a playwright but in a form that he rarely otherwise attempted. *Duologue* is a monologue – and everything about it is contained in that paradoxical phrase. Rosemary is alone in her big house in Hampstead; she has convinced herself and tries to convince everyone else that she is quite happy alone, but as the play goes on her longing for Gregory, her departed husband, steals upon her. She begins to inhabit his voice and to let his voice inhabit her. Sensuously, daringly, at one point she stretches out on the sofa on which used to sleep: '*as if consciously committing a blasphemous act*', remarks Rattigan, noting the morbid eroticism of her longing (p. 116). A thread of sexual implication runs through the piece: she ventriloquises Gregory discussing their sex life, making clear his rejected advances, his masturbation, their rows and (what we would now call) 'make-up sex' (p. 119).

It's a play that works through absence. The absence of Rosemary's interlocutor, the absence of her feelings, the literal absence of another actor onstage. The television production uses several point-of-view shots of the sofa, and we half-expect the husband to appear, to be willed into existence. Onstage, it is more complex; we are used to a stage convention of someone speaking to an unseen interlocutor, so there is some ambivalence about whether Gregory is there or not. Her tenderness towards him, the aching eroticism of lying in his place, is therefore amplified by the stage image, and gives even more power to her yearning for her husband. Towards the end of the monologue, she seems to have persuaded herself that it is her husband's spirit speaking through her and she asks him to tell her if she killed him: 'Open a door, break a window, upset a table? Make me some sign!' (p. 121). There is silence and she makes one last plea, at which point the clock strikes midnight. But is that her answer? The clock would have struck anyway. Rosemary gets no resolution and the play, bleakly, leaves her lonelier than ever.

Early in the monologue, Rosemary reports on her book-group meeting at which she made a rather high-handed speech denouncing Kafka: 'Kafka strikes no chord on my piano. I'm afraid I don't believe in nameless fears. I believe that all fears can be named and once named can be exorcised' (p. 114). The ending of the play shows precisely how hollow that sentiment is. But note also that her hasty rejection of Kafka is an echo of a similar middle-class, middle-brow lady. In 1953, Rattigan characrerised 'Aunt Edna' as a woman who would say of Kafka 'so obscure, my dear, and why always look on the dark side of things?'[63] Here, Rattigan is making clear the inadequacy of such a view, in a world shadowed by loneliness and loss.

Rattigan had always been very close to his mother, yet for him she was also his Aunt Edna, a conservative, judgemental figure whom he struggled to defy. He had always been very careful to mask his homosexuality from her, but by the late sixties he stopped bothering, almost flaunting his sexuality. In some of his later plays, he perhaps draws portraits of his mother: in the imperious seaside tyrant Mrs Railton-Bell from *Separate Tables* (a play he dedicated to his mother) and the prudish, moralistic Edith Davenport in *Cause Célèbre*.[64] Rosemary Hodge is perhaps another portrait of a woman who professed to despise her husband in life – as Vera did Frank – but only came to understand her real feelings after his death and to accept the value of sexual desire. Finally, though, we might also see an image of Rattigan himself in Gregory. Rattigan was dying when he wrote *Duologue* and he knew it. I don't think it's too fanciful to detect a note in this play of a scorned playwright telling the world: you may not like me now, but you'll miss me when I'm gone.

Duologue, like *Who is Sylvia?*, is unique in Rattigan's work. Both plays take risks with dramaturgy, strike out in new directions. Both plays have tended to be marginalised by most readers of Rattigan's work. Publishing them together offers us an opportunity to see the range of Rattigan's work, as well as its depth, and his constant attempt to test the limits of his powers as a playwright.

DAN REBELLATO

Notes

1. See pp. xi-xiii of this volume.

2. Darlow, Michael. *Terence Rattigan: The Man and His Work*. London: Quartet, 2000, p. 235.

3. See my introduction to Terence Rattigan. *The Deep Blue Sea*. London: Nick Hern Books, 1999, pp. xviii-xxxvi.

4. Terence Rattigan. Letter to Rex Harrison. 15 February 1950. Rattigan Papers: British Library, Add. MSS. 74346 A.

5. File 74342 in the Rattigan archive in the British Library is described, based on the cover sheet, as amendments to *Who is Sylvia?* made in 1954 and sent to Roger Machell of Hamish Hamilton, Rattigan's publisher. But Hamish Hamilton had already published the play by 1954, both in an individual edition and in the second volume of the *Collected Plays*, so it is given more likely that Rattigan sent the manuscript of the final draft of the play to Machell as a gift but the cover page had remained in the archive. The contents of this file actually appear to be structural plans for Acts One and Three of the play, notes on theme and characters, and drafts of the first half of Act One and a few pages from Act Two. They offer an unusually vivid insight into Rattigan's thinking and creative processes but, perhaps because of being misdescribed in the catalogue, they have not been drawn on before, which is why I have quoted very fully from them. I shall refer to these papers as *The Search for May*.

6. *Green After April*'s second act is set in 1930.

7. His surname also changes, from Arbour to Green (explaining the punning title *Green After April*) to Wright, while it is his wife's given name that alters, from Isabel to Mary to Caroline. Mark's family title, Lord Binfield, is evidently a little nod to the area where he composed the first draft of the play.

8. *The Search for May*, p. 14. In these initial notes, Williams was imagined to be a woman housekeeper and Daphne was called Doris.

9. *Ibid.*, pp. 5-6. *Égalités* and *en plein* are terms from casino gambling: betting on *égalité* is a relatively safe bet while betting *en plain* is staking all on a single number or card.

10. *Ibid.*, p. 26.

11. Terence Rattigan. Letter to Rex Harrison. *op. cit.*

12. Quoted in Darlow, *op. cit.*, p. 257.

13. *Ibid.*, p. 256. Frank had four months of military service in France and Belgium during the First World War before being invalided out, and wrung every drop of use out of his military title. In *Who is Sylvia?*, it is Oscar who adopts the title 'Major' to attract women. (Later, of course, in *Separate Tables*, Rattigan would create another bogus major with a different kind of roving eye.)

14. *The Search for May*, *op. cit.* p. 6.

15. Geoffrey Wansell's biography contains the fanciful suggestion that Frank was forced out of the Diplomatic Service after an affair with Princess Elisabeth of Romania (*Terence Rattigan*. London: 4th Estate, 1995, p. 23). Michael Darlow's biography (rightly I think) pours cold water on this suggestion, identifying Terry as the source of the rumour, dramatising his father's behaviour to a schoolmate (*op. cit.*, p. 51).

16. Wansell *op. cit.*, p. 204; Darlow, *op. cit.*, p. 256.

17. *The Search for May*, *op. cit.*, p. 7.

18. Darlow, *op. cit.*, p. 131.

19. Quoted in Dan Rebellato. *1956 and All That: The Making of Modern Theatre*. London: Routledge, 1999, p. 195. That section (pp. 193–200) gives

much more information about the pervasive influence of psychoanalysis in thinking about homosexuality at the time.

20. Terence Rattigan. *The Man Who Loved Redheads*. 1954. Rattigan Papers: British Library. Add. MSS. 74345, p. 8.

21. Oscar Wilde in *The Importance of Being Earnest* (1895) and Emlyn Williams in *Accolade* (1950) also explore the 'double life' theme. It may not be coincidental that both playwrights were themselves bisexual. Williams's play opened only a month or so before Rattigan's, and the passing affinity of the two plays was noted by the critics.

22. Darlow, *op. cit.*, p. 257.

23. When Rattigan completed a draft of the play, he read it aloud to his mother and father, who reportedly 'laughed until the tears ran down their faces' (*ibid.*, p. 257), not the reaction that would have greeted a play continued in the vein of the first draft.

24. Glen Byam Shaw. Letter to Terence Rattigan. 10 February 1950. Rattigan Papers: British Library, Add. MSS. 74346 A.

25. *Inadmissible Evidence* by John Osborne uses the same device – three different characters played by the same actress – to emphasise the main character's mental confusions. After seeing and reading the play in 1969, Rattigan wrote to Osborne 'I have to tell you that I think it not only your fullest and most moving work, but the best play of the century' (quoted in John Heilpern. *John Osborne: A Patriot For Us*. London: Chatto & Windus, 2006, p. 192). Intriguingly, too, Osborne's 1964 play begins with the play's anti-hero being forced to defend himself in a High Court of his own imagination. Earlier that year, Rattigan's preface to the third volume of his *Collected Plays* is the playwright being cross-examined in a court filled, it seems, by his own characters, including Sir Robert Morton and Aunt Edna. The links between Osborne and Rattigan may be closer than generally acknowledged.

26. Terence Rattigan. Letter to A.D. Peters. 5 February 1950. Rattigan Papers: British Library, Add. MSS. 74346 A.

27. A.D. Peters. Letter to Terence Rattigan. 7 February 1950. *Ibid.*

28. Terence Rattigan. Letter to A.D. Peters. 8 February 1950. *Ibid.*

29. A.D. Peters. Letter to Terence Rattigan. 11 February 1950. *Ibid.*

30. Terence Rattigan. Letter to Harold Freedman. 10 February 1950. *Ibid.* Michael Darlow adds a third explanation for the cooling of their relationship. A former lover of Terry's, John Montgomery, was now working for Peters and mentioned over dinner that he was friendly with Kenneth Morgan and his new lover, and that they had all socialised together. Rattigan appears to have considered this a betrayal, and Montgomery blames this for Rattigan distancing himself from Peters' agency (Darlow *op. cit.*,

31. Harold Freedman. Letter to Terence Rattigan. 9 February 1950. Rattigan Papers: British Library, Add. MSS. 74346 A.

32. *Ibid.*

33. Rex Harrison. Letter to Terence Rattigan. [Arrived] 14 February 1950. *Ibid.*

34. Terence Rattigan. Letter to Rex Harrison. 15 February 1950. *Ibid.*

35. Harold Freedman. Telegram to Terence Rattigan. 18 February 1950. *Ibid.* In the event, *The King and I* went ahead without Rex Harrison as the King, to, I would suggest, the lasting benefit of the show.

36. Telegrams between Rex Harrison and Terence Rattigan. 4–9 March 1950. *Ibid.*

37. Michael Wilding. Letter to Terence Rattigan. 8 May 1950. *Ibid.*

38. John Mills. Letter to Terence Rattigan. 2 May 1950. *Ibid.*

39. Tennents. Letter to Terence Rattigan. 28 April 1950. *Ibid.*

40. Robert Flemyng. Letter to Terence Rattigan. 8 May 1950. *Ibid.*

41. Athene Seyler. Telegram to Tennents. 5 July 1950. *Ibid.*

42. Quoted in Tennents. Letter to Terence Rattigan. 29 May 1950. *Ibid.*

43. Terence Rattigan. Telegram to Harold Freedman. 1 June 1950. *Ibid.*

44. Quoted in John Barber. 'Hyde and seek – with Terence Rattigan'. *Daily Express.* 25 October 1950.

45. Juliet Duff. Letter to Terence Rattigan. 19 October 1950. Rattigan Papers: British Library, Add. MSS. 74346 A.

46. Quoted in Wansell, *op. cit.*, p. 211.

47. Robert Flemyng. Letter to Terence Rattigan. [Undated.] Rattigan Papers: British Library, Add. MSS. 74346 A.

48. Darlow, *op. cit.*, pp. 209-10.

49. H. H. H. 'New Rattigan Comedy: French Leave Without Tears?' *Cambridge Daily News*, 10 October 1950. Rattigan Papers: British Library, Add. MSS. 74553.

50. *The Times.* 25 October 1950, p. 6. In print the phrase is 'serious attention', which I take to be an error and so have amended.

51. *Daily Mail.* 25 October 1950; Beverley Baxter MP. 'This will not do, Mr Rattigan'. *Evening Standard*, 27 October 1950. In: Production File: *Who is Sylvia?*, Criterion Theatre, October 1950, V&A Blythe House Archive.

52. Alan Dent. 'Rattigan gives us a sad smile'. *News Chronicle.* 25 October 1950. Rattigan Papers: British Library, Add. MSS. 74553.

53. Quoted in Wansell, *op. cit.*, p. 211.

54. Harold Hobson. 'A Failure by Keats, a Hit by Terence Rattigan'. *Christian Science Monitor.* 6 Jan 1951. Rattigan Papers: British Library, Add. MSS. 74553.

55. Harold Freedman. Letter to Terence Rattigan. 28 March 1950. Rattigan Papers: British Library, Add. MSS. 74346 A.

56. *Today's Cinema.* 13 January 1955. Rattigan Papers: British Library, Add. MSS. 74553.

57. Darlow, *op. cit.*, p. 260.

58. The production can be viewed on *The Terence Rattigan Collection.* 2 Entertain, 2011. DVD.

59. Stanley Richards, ed. *The Best Short Plays 1970.* New York: Chilton, 1970. There was also discussion with Warner Brothers about a possible American television production but this seems not to have come to anything. Rattigan Papers: British Library, Add. MSS. 74471.

60. Alan Bryce. Letter to Michael Imison. 30 October 1974. Rattigan Papers: British Library, Add. MSS. 74471.

61. [Untitled article.] *Sunday Times.* 1 February 1976. Production File: *The Browning Version*, King's Head Theatre, January 1976, V&A Blythe House Archive.

62. He toyed with the rather unmellifluous name 'Rosemary Bartlethwaite' in the manuscript of *Duologue*. Rattigan Papers: British Library, Add. MSS. 74471.

63. Terence Rattigan. *The Collected Plays of Terence Rattigan: Volume Two.* London: Hamish Hamilton, 1953, p. xii.

64. See my introduction to Terence Rattigan. *Cause Célèbre*. London: Nick Hern Books, 2011, pp. xxvi–xxvii for a detailed account of Edith's resemblance to Vera.

List of Rattigan's Produced Plays

TITLE	BRITISH PREMIERE	NEW YORK PREMIERE
First Episode (with Philip Heimann)	Q Theatre, Kew, 11 Sept 1933 (transferred to Comedy Theatre, 26 Jan 1934	Ritz Theatre, 17 Sept 1934
French Without Tears	Criterion Theatre, 6 Nov 1936	Henry Miller Theatre, 28 Sept 1937
After the Dance	St James's Theatre, 21 June 1939	
Follow My Leader (with Anthony Maurice, alias Tony Goldschmidt)	Apollo Theatre, 16 Jan 1940	
Grey Farm (with Hector Bolitho)		Hudson Theatre, 3 May 1940
Flare Path	Apollo Theatre, 13 Aug 1932	Henry Miller Theatre, 23 Dec 1942
While the Sun Shines	Globe Theatre, 24 Dec 1943	Lyceum Theatre, 19 Sept 1944
Love in Idleness	Lyric Theatre, 20 Dec 1944	Empire Theatre (as *O Mistress Mine*), 23 Jan 1946
The Winslow Boy	Lyric Theatre, 23 May 1946	Empire Theatre, 29 Oct 1947
Playbill (*The Browning Version* and *Harlequinade*)	Phoenix Theatre, 8 Sept 1948	Coronet Theatre, 12 Oct 1949
Adventure Story	St James's Theatre, 17 March 1949	
A Tale of Two Cities (from Charles Dickens, with John Gielgud)	St Brendan's College Dramatic Society, Clifton, 23 Jan 1950	
Who is Sylvia?	Criterion Theatre, 24 Oct 1950	

Final Test (TV)	BBC TV, 29 July 1951	
The Deep Blue Sea	Duchess Theatre, 6 Mar 1952	Morosco Theatre, 5 Nov 1952
The Sleeping Prince	Phoenix Theatre, 5 Nov 1953	Coronet Theatre, 1 Nov 1956
Seperate Tables (*The Table by the Window* and *Table Number Seven*)	St James's Theatre, 22 Sept 1954	Music Box Theatre, 25 Oct 1956
Variation on a Theme	Globe Theatre, 8 May 1958	
Ross	Theatre Royal Haymarket 12 May 1960	Eugene O'Neill Theatre 26 Dec 1961
Joie de Vivre (with Robert Stolz and Paul Dehn)	Queen's Theatre, 14 July 1960	
Heart to Heart (TV)	BBC TV, 6 Dec 1962	
Man and Boy	Queen's Theatre, 4 Sept 1963	Brooks Atkinson Theatre, 12 Nov 1963
Ninety Years On (TV)	BBC TV, 29 Nov 1964	
Nelson – A Portrait in Miniature (TV)	Associated Television, 21 Mar 1966	
All On Her Own (TV) (adapted for the stage as *Duologue*)	BBC 2, 25 Sept 1968	
A Bequest to the Nation	Theatre Royal Haymarket 23 Sept 1970	
High Summer (TV)	Thames TV, 12 Sept 1972	
In Praise of Love (*After Lydia* and *Before Dawn*)	Duchess Theatre, 27 Sept 1973	Morosco Theatre, 10 Dec 1974
Cause Célèbre (radio)	BBC Radio 4, 27 Oct 1975	
Duologue	King's Head Theatre, 21 Feb 1976	
Cause Célèbre (stage)	Her Majesty's Theatre, 4 July 1977	
Less Than Kind	Jermyn Street Theatre, 20 January 2011	

WHO IS SYLVIA?

Who is Sylvia? was first produced at the Criterion Theatre, London, on 24 October 1950, with the following cast:

MARK	Robert Flemyng
WILLIAMS	Esmond Knight
DAPHNE	Diane Hart
SIDNEY	Alan Woolston
ETHEL	Diana Allen
OSCAR	Roland Culver
BUBBLES	Diana Hope
NORA	Diane Hart
DENIS	David Aylmer
WILBERFORCE	Roger Maxwell
DORIS	Diane Hart
CHLOE	Joan Benham
CAROLINE	Athene Seyler

Producer   Anthony Quayle
Set and Costume Designer   William Chappell

Characters

MARK
WILLIAMS
DAPHNE
SIDNEY
ETHEL
OSCAR
BUBBLES
NORA
DENIS
WILBERFORCE
DORIS
CHLOE
CAROLINE

ACT ONE
Summer 1917. About 8:00 p.m.

ACT TWO
Spring 1929. About 6:30 p.m.

ACT THREE
Winter 1950. About 6:00 p.m.

The action of the play passes in a flat in Knightsbridge.

ACT ONE

A first-floor flat in Knightsbridge. Large windows look on to a quiet street. Door backstage leads into hall, and another into bedroom. The room has an air of bachelor distinction, the furniture being considerably better chosen and displayed than the furnishings, which are rather drab and ordinary; some good pictures, mainly Dutch landscapes, a bronze head of a girl, not too conspicuously placed.

The time is about eight o'clock of a summer evening in 1917. The light has begun to fade but, as the curtain rises, we can see the dining table has been laid in the centre of the room, with two places. The room is empty.

There is the sound of the front door closing and after a moment MARK *enters. He is thirty-five and plainly goes to a tailor in or near Savile Row. He is wearing a dinner jacket, single-breasted, and a white waistcoat, and is carrying an object under his arm. This, as he removes the paper, is revealed to be a bottle of champagne, which he unwraps and places on the sideboard. Then he inspects the table, making a couple of meticulous changes. He next looks round the room, paying particular attention to the sofa, whose cushions he rearranges. Then, on a sudden impulse, he goes to the window and pulls the heavy curtains, leaving the room in darkness for a moment, until he turns on the lights. These, after a second's consideration, he dims discreetly. Then he rearranges a small vase of flowers on the table. He stands back and examines the effect, but not entirely satisfied, sits in one of the chairs at the table. Mouthing soundlessly he makes animated conversation to the other chair, and we see that he has to lean his head to one side to circumvent the flowers. He therefore removes the vase.*

Now, after a final glance round the room, he appears moderately satisfied. He takes a cigarette from a case, lights it, and goes briskly to a telephone.

MARK (*into telephone*). Hullo… I want Sloane 7838, please.
(*As he waits he still glances round the room.*) Cunliffe?…
Yes… Is Her Ladyship there?… Yes, please… Hullo,
darling… Darling, I'm afraid the most awful thing has just
happened. A long dispatch from Mesopotamia has just this
second come in, and it looks as if I won't be able to get home
till very late… Oh no, midnight, I should think, at the very
earliest. It might be much later than that, even… Who? Oh,
your father. Well, tell him how very sorry I am to miss him,
will you?… Oh no, darling, don't bother to do that – I'll have
a snack here in the office… Oh no, that's all right. One has to
get used to these things in wartime… Mesopotamia… Well,
it's the cypher they use, you see, one of the most complicated
there is in the world… Yes. Kiss Denis for me – tell him to be
good… Oh, did he? (*Submissively.*) Oh yes, darling, I quite
agree. Very naughty. Yes, darling. I'll talk to him in the
morning… Oh yes, very severe, I promise… I'm so sorry
about tonight… Goodnight. (*Rings off and jiggles the
telephone for the Exchange.*) Hullo… Are you there? Yes, I've
finished, thank you. I want Victoria 8440… Hullo, Foreign
Office? This is Lord St Neots. Who's in charge of the Middle
East department tonight? Well, it's a simple question, I should
have thought you could have given me a reasonably simple
answer… Look, dear lady, this is Lord St Neots. I work at the
Foreign Office. I have worked at the Foreign Office for the
past nine years. I simply want to know… Now how the
dickens can I identify myself on the telephone? I am Viscount
St Neots, the son of the Earl of Binfield. I am married. I have
one child, a boy, aged five, named Denis, and I live at No. 58
Belgrave Square. Now, dear lady, if there is anything else I
can tell you about myself I should be only too happy…
(*Furiously.*) Well, you can tell Mr Mole from me that he's a
blithering idiot. If I were a German spy I wouldn't go dashing
about ringing up the Foreign Office asking who's in charge of
the Middle East department. I'd jolly well know who was in
charge of the Middle East department. Come to think of it, I'd
probably *be* in charge of the Middle East department. (*Rather
pleased at this one, and chuckles appreciatively.*) Very well,
ring off, if you wish. I have said my say. (*Jiggles the*

telephone again.) Hullo, Exchange? Get me Victoria 8440 again, would you? I got cut off... (*In an assumed voice most inexpertly and suspiciously guttural*.) Hullo, Foreign Office. Please might with the Middle Eastern department to speak? Hullo, Middle East? (*In his normal voice*.) Who's in charge there tonight? Mr Seymour? Good. Put me on to him, would you... Charley? This is Mark – do me a little favour, would you? If my home rings up, I'm with you, deciphering a long dispatch about Mesopotamia, and can't talk for fear of dropping a stitch... What... That's better, isn't it? Gone out for a cup of coffee. You obviously have experience... No. I have none – honestly I haven't. First time in seven years. Believe it or not, it's true... No. Not ashamed of myself, yet. Tomorrow, perhaps. Not now... Oh, by the way, Charley, if my home should ring you'd better have this number, hadn't you. It's Sloane... Damn, I've forgotten it. I know it so well, too. No, it's not on the receiver... I tell you what. It's in the book under the name of Oscar Philipson – got that? Oscar Philipson, and the address is 12 Wilbraham Terrace, Knightsbridge... Yes, that's right. Thank you, Charley, I hope I shall be able to do the same for you one day... (*As an afterthought*.) Oh, by the way, give my best to your wife.

WILLIAMS, OSCAR PHILIPSON*'s manservant, enters. He is small, neat, rugged, and (for he is an ex-hatman) his 'sirs' and 'my lords' are military rather than domestic.*

WILLIAMS. Oh, you're here, my lord.

MARK. Hullo, Williams.

WILLIAMS. I didn't know. I was just going out. I hope everything's all right?

MARK (*rising*). Yes, thank you, Williams. Perfect, I think.

WILLIAMS. Of course, if you'd have let me know a bit earlier I could have made plans to stay in –

MARK. That's quite all right. As a matter of fact I'm very glad you're going out. I mean, it's kind enough of you to do what you have, anyway –

WILLIAMS. Oh, that's all right, my lord. I was glad of the chance, to be honest. One gets a bit fed up with nothing to do all day – just sitting alone there in the kitchen, waiting for the Captain's next leave –

MARK. Any news of him, Williams?

WILLIAMS. I had a line from him about a week ago – giving me notice as it happens – of course, joking, you know the Captain –

MARK. What had you done?

WILLIAMS. Well, in my last letter to him I said to him how I heard the war was going wonderfully and he'd be sure to be home for Christmas.

MARK. And Captain Philipson took umbrage, did he?

WILLIAMS. Well, out in France, as you know, things look a bit different to the way they do from here. I remember when I was on the Somme, just before I got my packet, I used to get proper fed up with letters from home, telling me how gloriously I was advancing when I'd been stuck in the same ruddy hole for three weeks.

MARK. I didn't know you were on the Somme – I just missed it.

WILLIAMS. Did you get a blighty?

MARK. No. I was only out there by kind permission of the Foreign Office; and last year they withdrew their kind permission – that's all.

WILLIAMS. I suppose you get white feathers?

MARK. Enough to stuff a pillow.

WILLIAMS. So do I. One old duck said to me yesterday on the Tube – 'Young man,' she said, 'why aren't you in uniform?' And I said, 'Because there's a ruddy war on, you silly old sausage.' Proper mad, she got. Called the conductor and all. (*Chuckles at the reminiscence.*) Well, my lord, is there anything more I can do for you, because I ought to be getting along?

MARK. No, thank you, Williams. I'm very grateful.

WILLIAMS. Oh – do you see I put the lady out for you?

MARK. The lady?

WILLIAMS. The bust.

    WILLIAMS *points to the bronze girl's head on the pedestal.*

MARK. Oh yes.

WILLIAMS. The Captain had it in the lumber room. If you ask me he's never properly appreciated it. I think it's beautiful.

MARK. Thank you, Williams.

WILLIAMS. Must be wonderful to be able to do things like that.

MARK. Oh, well, it's only a hobby, you know –

WILLIAMS. It ought to be more than a hobby, if you ask me. It ought to be an occupation. If I could sculpt or paint or something like that, I'd be at it all day long. Of course I've got my reading, but that isn't quite the same thing. (*Seeing the champagne.*) I see you brought the champagne. I know Captain Philipson would have been only too glad to have let you have one of his – (*Picking up champagne and putting it in ice bucket.*)

MARK. No. That would be stretching his hospitality too far. By the way, I've written to Captain Philipson telling him about tonight –

WILLIAMS. Yes, my lord.

MARK. Oh, and Williams. (*Slightly embarrassed.*) Just supposing I – er – got caught in a sudden storm, or something and – er – wanted to stay the night, would that be all right, do you think?

WILLIAMS. Yes, my lord, of course. Only too easy. The bed is made up.

MARK. Of course, I probably won't be needing it at all –

WILLIAMS. You never know, my lord. It's very hot tonight. I should say there's a good deal of thunder in the air. Just leave a note for me, would you, so I'll know.

MARK. Yes, I will. Oh, Williams – just in case I don't see you to thank you – (*Takes out his wallet.*)

WILLIAMS. No, my lord, there's no need to do that.

MARK *gives him a pound.*

Oh, well – that's very kind of you, I'm sure.

MARK. Going out with your girl?

WILLIAMS. I haven't got a girl. Not steady, that is. I don't hold with it.

MARK. Don't hold with going steady?

WILLIAMS. No, my lord. It's bad for a man's morale, getting tied up to one woman all his life – at least that's the way I see it. It eats into his soul – makes him old before his time.

MARK. Williams – you're speaking to a married man.

WILLIAMS. Oh, well – *chacun à son goût*, as they say. Mind you, I'm not saying there's not a lot to be said for the blessed state – provided you don't let it get you down. But too many married men do, and there's the trouble.

MARK. I think there's something in what you say, Williams –

WILLIAMS. It's not so much me that says it, my lord, as H.G. Wells. Very illuminating, Wells.

There is a knock at the front door.

MARK. My God! That must be my guest.

WILLIAMS. Hope she hasn't been ringing long. You can never hear the bell from here. I'll let her in.

MARK (*distractedly*). No. I think perhaps you'd better let me do that, Williams, if you don't mind. You see, I haven't had time yet to explain to her about this flat – I merely gave her this address.

WILLIAMS. Oh. Doesn't she know who you are, my lord?

MARK. No. I haven't actually told her my name yet.

WILLIAMS. Well, what name have you told her?

MARK. Damn it, man, I haven't told her any name. We just don't happen yet to know each other awfully well, that's all. It takes such an infernally short time for a bus to get from Whitehall to Hyde Park Corner.

WILLIAMS. Ah. One of those. I see, my lord. Well, I'll just slip along to the kitchen and when you've let her in I'll nip out.

MARK. Yes, do. (*Starts for hall, then turns back.*)

Another knock at the front door.

Williams! You think a name is advisable –

WILLIAMS. Oh. Very highly.

MARK. What do you suggest?

WILLIAMS (*after considering*). The Captain uses Mason a lot.

MARK. I don't like Mason. Too rugged. What about Robinson?

WILLIAMS. You don't look a Robinson.

MARK. Smith?

WILLIAMS. No. That's fatal. (*After considering.*) Featherstonhaugh?

MARK. Don't be idiotic.

A third knock.

My God – she'll go in a second. I know – Wright. How do you like that? Rather good, isn't it? Wright it shall be.

WILLIAMS. Yes, my lord. I mean, very good, Mr Wright. *Bonne chance.*

They disappear, MARK *in the lead. After a pause we hear the front door closing and voices in the hall.*

MARK (*off*). I hope you found it all right.

DAPHNE (*off*). Oh, yes. Quite easy really, only two stops in the Tube from Notting Hill.

DAPHNE enters, ushered in by MARK. *She is in the early twenties and her face, partly concealed under a terrible hat – for she is not in evening dress – bears a marked resemblance to the bronze head. Her accent might be described as cautious.*

Oh, look at you in evening dress. You are awful. You said not to –

MARK. Well – only a dinner jacket, you know. Doesn't really count.

She looks round the room.

DAPHNE (*rapturously*). Oh, pictures! I love pictures, don't you? Of course, I can see you do. Oh, we've got one just I like that at home. (*Stands in front of a picture gazing at it with the eye of a connoisseur.*)

MARK (*behind her*). That one's by a Dutch painter.

DAPHNE. Oh, is it? (*Gazes at it.*) Of course, the colours are different in ours and there are more cows. It's called *Dawn on the Highlands*. Who would that be by, do you think?

MARK. Well – it could be by quite a lot of people.

DAPHNE (*a shade scornfully*). I must ask Mr Fortescue. He'll know. Mr Fortescue's my boss at the office. He's wonderful really. He knows everything there is to know about everything.

MARK. He sounds wonderful.

DAPHNE. He is. (*In a confidential murmur.*) I say, old bean, where's the oojah?

MARK. The oojah?

DAPHNE. The om-tiddly-om-pom.

MARK *still looks baled.*

The umpti-poo.

MARK (*light breaking*). Oh, the umpti-poo. How foolish of me. It's through this door here, and then on the right. (*Opens the bedroom door.*)

DAPHNE (*as she passes him*). You didn't mind me asking, did you, old fruit? I do think a girl should be modernistic these days, don't you?

MARK (*with enthusiasm*). I quite agree. As modernistic as she can possibly be.

DAPHNE *goes out.* MARK *goes to the sideboard and starts to undo the caviar. There is a discreet knock at the hall door.* WILLIAMS *then opens it.*

WILLIAMS. She's in there, isn't she?

MARK. That's right. The oojah.

WILLIAMS. I saw the light on. I brought this, some nice hot toast for the caviar.

He comes to the table with it.

MARK. Thank you very much, Williams.

WILLIAMS. I say, I got a squint at her coming in. Do you know, my lord, who she's the living spittin' image of?

MARK. No. Who?

WILLIAMS. That girl there. (*Points at the bronze head.*)

MARK. Oh! Do you think so?

WILLIAMS. Not a doubt of it. In fact, I thought perhaps she'd sat to you for it. She didn't, did she?

MARK. No, Williams. No one sat to me for that.

WILLIAMS. From imagination, was it?

MARK. From memory.

WILLIAMS. Who of?

MARK. Of a girl I knew once.

WILLIAMS. Um, terrible hat. Never make the best of themselves, do they?

MARK. Very rarely. (*Nervously.*) Er – Williams – don't you think –

WILLIAMS. That's all right, my lord. She's still there. I can see the light from here. As I was saying, it's wonderful what these girls do to themselves in the name of beauty. Now the Captain's got a friend – his latest – Ethel – have you met her, my lord?

MARK (*distrait*). I don't know, Williams. So many of the Captain's friends seem to be called Ethel.

WILLIAMS. You couldn't mistake *this* Ethel. What she puts on herself you wouldn't hardly believe. Holy terror, she is – least, not so holy, I suppose, but a terror all right. I remember once – look out, my lord. Lights are off. *Vive le sport.*

He disappears through the doors and closes them gently after him. After a moment DAPHNE *comes through the bedroom door.*

MARK. Oh, hullo.

DAPHNE. Is that your garden, out there?

MARK. What? Oh yes. It belongs to this flat.

DAPHNE. Nice having a garden – especially this weather.

MARK. We might sit out there, later.

DAPHNE. Yes. That'd be nice. How do you get to it?

MARK. From the bedroom.

DAPHNE. Oh. (*After a faint pause.*) Yes. That'd be very nice.

MARK. Look, shall we sit down? I'm afraid it's only cold, you know. The fact is this is my man's night out.

DAPHNE (*seating herself*). Terrible the servant problem these days, isn't it? It's all this Bolshevism about.

MARK, *having seated her, helps her to caviar, with some ceremony.* DAPHNE *watches it going on the plate with bewilderment, but is too polite to ask what it is.*

MARK. Yes. I expect so.

DAPHNE (*inspecting the caviar cautiously*). It's funny – you wouldn't really expect the Russians to go and abdicate their Tsar like that, after all these years, would you? On the other hand, you've got to see two sides to every question, haven't you, and there's no doubt that he'd rather been asking for it, carrying on the way he has all this time, and Rasputin and all that. And then, of course, there's always social economics, isn't there, eh?

MARK. I'm so sorry. I didn't quite follow –

DAPHNE. I was giving my views on what's happened in Russia.

MARK. Oh, I see. Yes. I cordially agree. There's always social economics –

He has been trying to open the champagne. He now succeeds.

Ah. There we are.

He pours some into her glass and into his own.

DAPHNE. Ooh. Lovely! Sparkling gigglewasser.

MARK. I beg your pardon?

DAPHNE. It's a name for champagne. Giggle-water, you see, and then the German for water being wasser, it becomes gigglewasser.

MARK. But this isn't German champagne.

DAPHNE. I never said it was, silly. It's just a name Mr Fortescue invented for champagne –

MARK. Oh, I see. Mr Fortescue. (*Sits down opposite her.*) Er – this is Lanson '04.

DAPHNE *takes a sip.*

DAPHNE (*at length*). So it is. '04. Fancy.

MARK *looks at her but says nothing. He notices that she is not eating and divines the cause.*

MARK. I do hope you like the caviar. If you don't, I can assure you that Messrs Fortnum and Mason will answer for it with their lives.

DAPHNE *lets out a merry peal of laughter.* MARK *looks pleased that his little joke has gone down so well.*

DAPHNE. You sounded just like Mr Fortescue when you said that.

The smile fades from MARK*'s face.*

MARK. Oh! Did I?

DAPHNE. Shall I let you into a little secret? This is my very first taste of caviar.

MARK. Well, there has to be a first time for everything, doesn't there? Toast?

DAPHNE. Practically everything. (*Attacking some caviar with a spoon.*) Well, here goes. (*Takes a mouthful and patently finds it distasteful. But recovers quickly.*) It's quite nice, really, isn't it?

MARK. I think so. (*Holds up his glass.*) Here's to a pair of the most beautiful eyes I've ever seen on any human being in all my life –

DAPHNE. Quite the Oscar Wilde, aren't you? (*Takes a sip and giggles.*)

MARK (*rises*). Look, I'm afraid you're not enjoying that caviar very much –

DAPHNE. Well, now you mention it, I never was much of a one for fishy things.

MARK. Then let's pass on to the next course. (*Removes the plates.*)

DAPHNE. Seems a pity, though – it's awfully expensive, isn't it?

MARK. Oh, well. Expense is only a relative term, isn't it?

DAPHNE. Oh yes. Absolutely relative, isn't it?

He places the next course before her.

Oh, chicken. Now that *is* nice.

MARK. I'm glad we're on safer ground with chicken. (*Begins to pour her another glass of champagne.*)

DAPHNE. Oh no. Stop. I don't want to get squiffy. You don't know how I carry on when I'm squiffy.

MARK. No, I don't. But I should very much like to.

DAPHNE (*looking up at him*). I might do things I might regret.

MARK (*seductively*). You might regret them. But would I?

DAPHNE. You've really quite a way with you, haven't you? Oh, well – just up to there –

She indicates the spot on the glass to which MARK *is permitted to pour.*

Whoa! That's lovely. Well. (*Extending her glass.*)

Here's to living, here's to dying,
Here's to laughing, here's to crying,
Here's to this and here's to that,
But chiefly here's to that.

MARK. One of Mr Fortescue's?

DAPHNE. Yes. How did you guess?

He puts the champagne in the ice bucket, then returns to the table and resumes his seat.

MARK. I've no idea. (*Extending his glass.*) Now I'll give you a toast. I'll just say – Here's to love –

DAPHNE *giggles. There is an appreciable pause while both get on with the business of eating.*

DAPHNE. You know, I don't know very much about you, do I? I don't even know your name.

MARK. Don't you?

DAPHNE. What is it?

MARK. Mark.

DAPHNE. Mark? (*After a second's reflection.*) Yes, I like that.

MARK. Do you? I'm so glad.

DAPHNE (*firmly*). It's a *nice* name, Mark. What's your surname?

MARK, *in the act of taking a sip of wine, coughs. He takes rather more time to recover than seems necessary. From his expression of acute concentration, it is fairly plain that he has forgotten his chosen pseudonym.*

MARK (*at length*). Well, now – why don't you guess?

DAPHNE. Well, it could be almost anything, couldn't it?

MARK. Yes. Indeed it could.

DAPHNE (*a shade scornfully*). It's not Smith, is it?

MARK. Oh no. It's definitely not Smith. I hate Smith.

DAPHNE. Yes, it is rather common, isn't it?

MARK (*desperately*). I love *your* name. Now, Daphne Prentice is a charming name –

DAPHNE. Oh. I'm glad you think so. I always do think it's rather *nice* – though I say it who shouldn't.

MARK. Exquisite. It has music… I know – Wright!

DAPHNE. I beg your pardon?

MARK (*easily*). Wright. Mark Wright. That's my name. Do you like that?

DAPHNE. No.

MARK (*with a slight laugh*). Oh dear. Why not?

DAPHNE. I just don't think it's very nice, that's all.

MARK (*a shade defiantly*). Well, what other name *would* you have thought nice?

He glances at the door.

Featherstonhaugh?

DAPHNE. Oh, no. That's silly.

MARK. I cordially agree.

There is a pause.

DAPHNE (*meditatively*). Percy Pennyfeather's nice, don't you think?

MARK. Yes, I suppose it is. And so is Fortescue. But you know, Daphne, quite honestly, I don't think that either of them are really as nice as Wright. Just have another sip of champagne, and you'll see how nice Wright is. Go on.

She does so, and lowers her glass. MARK *instantly pours more champagne into it.*

DAPHNE. Oh, you are awful, aren't you?

MARK. There. Now, doesn't Wright sound better to you?

DAPHNE. Yes, it does, in a way. It rather grows on you, doesn't it? Mark Wright. Mark Wright. It's straightforward anyhow.

MARK. Simple and honest and direct, isn't it? No frills about it. Mark Wright. I must say I like it myself very much indeed. Mark Wright. (*Takes a sip of champagne in silent toast to his new name.*)

DAPHNE. What do you do for a living?

MARK *puts his glass down carefully.*

MARK. Well, why don't you have another guess?

DAPHNE. I say, old bean, you do like guessing games, don't you?

MARK. After all, there aren't nearly so many occupations as there are names. (*An idea has struck him at the word 'occupations'.*) You really ought to be able to guess my occupation, Daphne.

DAPHNE *is reluctant to try.*

All right, I'll put you out of your misery. I'm a sculptor.

DAPHNE. A sculptor?

There is a pause while DAPHNE *wrinkles her brows in thought.*

MARK (*anxiously*). You think that's nice, don't you?

DAPHNE *still ponders for a moment.*

DAPHNE (*at length*). Yes, I do. I think it's quite nice.

MARK. Splendid.

DAPHNE. What sort of things do you sculpture?

MARK. Well – (*Rises and crosses to bronze head.*) That, for example.

DAPHNE (*turning her head*). That? (*Gazes at it in silence.*)

MARK (*anxiously again*). Nice, don't you think?

DAPHNE (*peering*). I can't see it properly.

MARK. I'll get it for you.

He brings the head over and places it on the table. DAPHNE *gazes at it.*

DAPHNE. Who is it?

MARK. Just a girl.

DAPHNE. Oh. No one special?

MARK. On the contrary. Someone very special. Don't you think she looks like you?

DAPHNE. Well, I don't know that I feel altogether flattered, I must say.

MARK (*a shade sharply*). Well, you should. If you don't it's my fault. She was very beautiful.

DAPHNE. 'Was'? Is she dead?

MARK. No. Only she probably doesn't look anything like this now. This is how I remembered her as she was – let me see now – I was seventeen then and I'm thirty-two now – fifteen years ago – (*Lost in reverie as he gazes at the head.*)

DAPHNE. Go on. Tell me about her –

MARK. There's very little to tell, I'm afraid. You'd be disappointed.

DAPHNE. Oh no. That's all right. I love a story.

MARK. Well, I was seventeen, as I told you. She was sixteen. I met her – of all places – at a garden party. The young people were forced to play tennis. Our hostess made us partners, this girl and I – and we played rather well together, although heaven knows I was never any good at the damn game. We won: 6:3, 6:2. After that we went for a walk together, not very far or for very long, because we both knew our parents were hating the party and would be wanting to go home soon. At a certain spot where there was a stile and a dead tree she let me kiss her – just once – and then we went back to the party. On the way home we talked about opera. I dropped her with her parents and that was the last I ever saw of her. A month later I heard she'd gone with her family to South Africa, and she's been there ever since. She married a man called Willoughby-Grant, and they live near Capetown. A very pleasant house, somebody told me – right by the sea.

He stops. DAPHNE *looks at him, bewildered.*

DAPHNE. Is that all the story?

MARK. Yes. That's all.

DAPHNE. Well, really, I must say. I see what you mean about my being disappointed –

MARK. You like stories with more action?

DAPHNE. Well, I like them to have a happy ending, anyway.

MARK (*smiling at her*). Perhaps this one has a happy ending.

There is a pause, broken by the ringing of the telephone.

Oh, damn! (*Gets up.*) Excuse me. (*Goes to the telephone. Into telephone.*) Hullo?... Yes... Right, thank you, Charley. (*Rings off, then stands in doubt and apprehension, looking at* DAPHNE.) Er – look; Daphne – I wonder if I could ask you to do something.

DAPHNE (*ever cautious*). Rather depends what 'it' is, doesn't it?

MARK. Yes. But this isn't very difficult. Would you mind awfully leaving me alone while I make this telephone call – it's very confidential, you see.

DAPHNE. Confidential? Oh, well – that's quite all right. (*Gets up.*) You give me suspicions, you know –

MARK. What suspicions?

DAPHNE. I'll tell you later. (*Goes into the bedroom.*)

MARK *lifts the telephone.*

MARK. Sloane 7838, please... (*Waits for the answer in some evident trepidation, but when he speaks, his voice is certainly solicitous.*) Hullo, darling. Did you ring me? I was out having a cup of coffee and a bun... Oh, plodding ahead, you know, plodding ahead. Who?... Your father?... Oh, does he? All right... Oh, good evening, sir... What? Full moon? Yes, I think there is... Why?... Zeppelins. Oh no, sir. The zeppelin threat, I assure you, is now finally over... Cellar? Oh, no sir. The boy is perfectly safe where he is unless there is an alarm... But he's not afraid of the zeppelins. As a matter of fact I happen to know he even enjoys the zeppelins... Well, sir, why not? Searchlights in the sky and a lot of lovely bangs, what more can any child want?... I'm not being callous, sir, Denis told me himself... Yes, he told me that Nanny makes him put in his prayers 'God keep the zeppelins away' and he cheats every night and says under his breath 'God don't you do anything of the kind'... (*Alarmed.*) No,

sir, you mustn't... It's not blasphemy... No, sir, please don't.
Please don't say a word to him. He wouldn't understand...
Well, yes, if they do come, but you can take it from me they
won't... Goodnight.

*He rings off, and is evidently a little put out by the
conversation. A trifle abstractedly he opens the bedroom
door, and calls.*

It's all right now. I'm finished.

DAPHNE *comes back. He holds her chair for her as she sits.*

I'm so sorry for the interruption.

DAPHNE. No trouble at all, I assure you.

MARK. Excuse me, a moment.

*He goes to the window and, taking care of the blackout,
peeps through the curtains.*

DAPHNE *watches him steadily.*

I just wanted to see if there were any searchlights on.

DAPHNE. Got wind of something?

MARK (*with his head through the curtains*). No, not 'wind'
exactly. Just something that was said on the telephone a
moment ago, made me think of it. Not a sign of anything, as
I thought. (*Comes back from the window.*)

While MARK *is arranging the next course,* DAPHNE *is
staring hard at him.*

DAPHNE. Of course, now I don't just suspect, I think I know –

MARK *turns nervously with trifle poised.*

MARK. Know what?

DAPHNE. You're thirty-two, you're not in uniform, sculptors
aren't exempt I wouldn't suppose, and anyway, no one's ever
made a living at just sculpture –

MARK. Oh, surely. Some people have, haven't they? Rodin, for
instance –

DAPHNE. Champagne and caviar?

MARK *places the dish before her.*

MARK. Oh, I should think so.

DAPHNE (*scornfully*). Don't tell me! I know the way artistical people live, and it's not like this. No, there's something else you don't want me to know about, but you needn't fuss, because I do.

MARK. Oh?

DAPHNE. You're Secret Service, aren't you?

MARK. Well –

DAPHNE (*interrupting*). That's all right, dear. I know you're not allowed to tell.

MARK (*after a pause*). You think that Secret Service agents live on champagne and caviar?

DAPHNE. Oh yes, of course. Ever so well paid, I should think – what with the danger and all –

MARK (*lightly*). Oh, I don't know there's all that much danger, you know. Just a job, like any other.

DAPHNE. Don't tell me! I know what goes on. Well, it's really quite a thrill, isn't it? (*Gazes at him in awe and wonder.*)

MARK. You think spies are nice?

DAPHNE. Oh, *you're* not a spy. Germans are spies. British are agents. (*Continues to gaze at him, not touching her food.*)

MARK. Look, you're not eating your trifle –

DAPHNE. Oh, I couldn't. I couldn't touch another thing. Excitement always gets me like that, you know – it goes straight to my stomach.

MARK. Oh, I'm so sorry. (*Gets up and hovers over her, a shade conscience-stricken.*) Look, supposing I were to tell you –

DAPHNE (*stopping her ears*). Oh no – you mustn't tell me a thing. Not a thing. I know it's wrong. They shoot you for it.

He looks down at her in doubt. She smiles up at him. He gently takes her hands off her ears.

MARK. You don't have to stop your ears to what I'm going to tell you now, Daphne. I think you're the most enchanting and attractive and adorable creature in the world and if you would allow me to, I could be very, very fond of you.

DAPHNE (*gently*). Saucy, aren't you?

She closes her eyes and puts her head back in undisguised invitation. MARK avails himself of it gently, at first, and then with warmth.

MARK (*murmuring*). Daphne – my darling Daphne –

There is a sudden sharp noise at the window, as of a stone being thrown.

What was that?

DAPHNE. Sounded like a stone at the window.

There is the sound of a voice calling 'Hi!' from the street outside.

Someone shouting too.

DAPHNE *rises.*

SIDNEY (*off*). Hi!

MARK *crosses room quickly and goes to the window.*

MARK. Hullo, what is it?

SIDNEY (*off*). Is anyone there?

MARK. What?

SIDNEY (*off*). I'm looking for Daphne Prentice.

MARK. I can't hear.

MARK draws the curtains and opens the window. The light has now gone from the sky.

(*Out of the window.*) What do you want?

SIDNEY (*off. In shrill, cockney tones*). I been ringing the bell and nothing happened.

MARK. Well, who are you? Go away!

SIDNEY (*off*). Is Daphne in there? Daph? Are you in there?

DAPHNE (*in alarm*). Goodness gracious! It's Sidney.

MARK. Who's Sidney?

DAPHNE. My young brother. Oh, dear! I wonder what it is. Could you let him in, Mr Wright?

MARK. I suppose so.

He leans out of window.

Here, catch.

He throws a bunch of keys.

The big one's the downstairs door. It's Flat No. 2 on the first floor.

SIDNEY (*off*). Right-ho!

DAPHNE. Well, I never. What could he be wanting?

MARK. I suppose he's not expecting to come to supper too, is he?

DAPHNE. Well, I don't know, I'm sure. Perhaps everyone's out at home and he felt lonely –

MARK. Oh, dear –

DAPHNE. Oh, he's such a clever little boy, doing ever so well for his age, Mr Wright. He's in munitions now.

MARK. Is he?

The front door is heard to slam.

Oh, there he is.

DAPHNE. You'll like him ever so much, I know.

MARK. I'm sure I shall.

MARK *opens doors.* SIDNEY *comes in, gives* MARK *his keys, then confronts* DAPHNE.

DAPHNE. Sidney! What are you doing here?

SIDNEY. Dad says you're to come home. Mum's back unexpected and she's creating –

DAPHNE (*angrily*). Oh, really! Isn't Mum awful! What – is she in one of her moods, or something?

SIDNEY. Terrible. She told Dad if he wasn't careful 'is daughter'd grow up an old tart like Auntie Mabel.

DAPHNE. Oh, Sidney, be quiet! (*Suddenly conscious of her social duties.*) Oh, Mr Wright, I'm so sorry, but I'm sure you understand about these little family squabbles. (*Tone changes as she turns back to her brother.*) Now listen, Sidney. You just go straight back to Mum and tell her she and Dad are making a fuss about nothing. Tell her I haven't even finished my dinner yet, and I'll come back when I'm ready and not before.

SIDNEY. Mum said I was to wait and see you home.

DAPHNE. That's ridiculous. Mr Wright will see me home – won't you, Mr Wright?

MARK. Of course.

SIDNEY. Mum said to remember what happened the last time, when Mr Pennyfeather saw you home.

DAPHNE. Oh, Sidney, really! (*Turns back to* MARK) Well, I don't know what to say, I'm sure, Mr Wright. It rather looks as if I shall have to go, I'm afraid.

MARK. Oh dear. I tell you what – I've got an idea. Why couldn't Sidney go back and say he hadn't been able to find the address?

SIDNEY. Cos it wouldn't be true.

MARK. You're a little lacking in creative imagination, aren't you?

DAPHNE. I really think I'd better go. Oh, it's ever so vexing. I am sorry. I'll get my hat. (*Goes into the bedroom.*)

MARK. Very well, my dear. If you must, you must, I suppose. Run and get a taxi, Sidney.

SIDNEY. What for?

MARK. To take your sister home in, of course.

SIDNEY. Who's going to pay for it?

MARK. *I* am going to pay for it.

SIDNEY. Why?

MARK (*taking* SIDNEY *out*). Never mind these abstruse questions of etiquette, Sidney. Just go and get that taxi. Turn right and right again and stand on the corner, until one passes.

DAPHNE *reappears from the bedroom.* MARK *comes back in.*

I've just sent Sidney for a taxi.

DAPHNE (*anxiously*). Oh, I do hope you didn't take seriously what Sidney let out about Mr Pennyfeather.

MARK. My dear, I can assure you, Mr Pennyfeather is the least of my worries at the moment. I'm only so upset that our evening should have ended so unsatisfactorily.

DAPHNE. Oh, well – there *are* other evenings, aren't there?

MARK. I hope so. Oh, indeed I hope so.

He kisses her.

Damn Sidney.

DAPHNE. It's Mum you should damn. Not little Sidney.

MARK. Having met little Sidney I prefer to damn little Sidney. (*Turns to the door.*) I'll just slip along to the kitchen and leave a note for the servant. (*At the door.*) I suppose we couldn't take two taxis, one for Sidney and one for ourselves?

DAPHNE. Well – it might took a little odd, mightn't it?

MARK. No odder than the other alternative, which is to take one taxi and put Sidney on the roof.

He goes out, leaving doors open.

DAPHNE, *left alone, heaves a sigh, then sits on the sofa dejectedly. A door slams off and a very vivid lady* (ETHEL) *appears, in evening dress of extremely daring style, and a face like an exotic mask. She has evidently opened the front door with a latchkey, because she is slipping it into her bag on entering. She nods pleasantly at* DAPHNE, *who has risen, alarmed at the apparition.*

ETHEL. Hot, isn't it?

DAPHNE. Yes, it is, isn't it. Quite sultry, really –

Her voice trails into astonished silence as she gazes at ETHEL, *who has wandered over to a cupboard which she now opens as from long practice and from which she brings a bottle of whisky and a tumbler. She pours out quite deliberately about a third of a tumblerful of the whisky, and then, with little finger genteelly curled, lifts her veil. Suddenly in one vast swallow she flings the drink down her gullet. No expression whatever crosses her countenance as she waits for a moment, savouring the drink. Then she politely holds out the bottle towards* DAPHNE.

ETHEL (*with eyebrows courteously raised*). Do you indulge?

DAPHNE. Oh no – thank you ever so.

ETHEL *nods pleasantly and pours herself out another vast drink. Holding it undrunk, at the moment, she wanders to the mantelpiece. Then she takes a cigarette from a box and prepares to light it.*

Excuse me asking, won't you – but would you mind telling me who you are?

ETHEL (*as if that explained everything*). Ethel.

DAPHNE. Oh. Well, I'm sorry, but I'm afraid you'll have to tell me more than that. Haven't you got a surname?

ETHEL (*after due thought*). Yes.

DAPHNE. What is it – if I might make so bold?

ETHEL. Skeffington-Rivers, I think. Yes. I'm almost sure it's that.

She flings back her drink, puts the glass and bottle back in the cupboard, and wanders to the bedroom door.

(*Conversationally.*) They say he went to Borneo.

She smiles vaguely and politely at DAPHNE *and drifts into the bedroom.*

DAPHNE (*aghast*). Well!

MARK *comes in from the hall.*

MARK. There we are, that's done.

DAPHNE. Well, really, Mr Wright, you have some very funny friends – I have to say.

MARK. Oh?

DAPHNE. Who was that woman who's just gone into your bedroom?

MARK. Has a woman just gone into my bedroom?

DAPHNE. Certainly. What's more she carried on as if she owned the whole flat – she had a latchkey, too –

MARK. Oh, did she tell you her name?

DAPHNE. Well – she didn't seem quite sure of her surname, but her Christian name was Ethel.

MARK. Ethel? Ethel? (*Suddenly realising.*) Oh, Lord! Ethel! (*After a moment of doubt, he laughs.*) That's easily explained. Ethel isn't my friend at all. In fact I've never met her –

DAPHNE. Then what's she doing wandering about your flat – making free with your whisky and –

MARK. She's a friend of Oscar Philipson. He's a friend of mine who usually stays here when he's on leave. I suppose he must have given her a latchkey.

DAPHNE. It's very careless of him, I must say. He's not on leave now, though, is he?

MARK. No, he's not. But I expect –

He breaks off as there comes a noise from the hall.

OSCAR (*off*). All right, cabby. No, don't bring them in. Stick them down there. My man will look after them. Goodnight. Thank you.

There is the sound of the front door slamming.

MARK. This only goes to show, my dear, how wrong one can sometimes be. It appears that Oscar Philipson is on leave.

OSCAR PHILIPSON *comes in. Three years older than* MARK*, he is dressed in the uniform* (*Captain's*) *of the Coldstream Guards.*

OSCAR (*with surprise*). Hullo, Mark. This is extremely good of you, I must say. How did you know?

MARK. I didn't know, that's just the trouble.

They shake hands.

(*Bitterly.*) Why on earth didn't you warn Williams?

OSCAR. Oh. Didn't I?

MARK. No, you didn't, you idiot. It's an absolutely lunatic way to behave, suddenly to arrive on leave in the middle of the night like this without warning anybody at all.

OSCAR. But it's not the middle of the night. It's 8:35 exactly. And anyway, I wired Ethel. Has she turned up?

MARK. Yes. She's in there.

OSCAR. Good.

MARK. But why did you only wire Ethel? Why didn't you wire me?

OSCAR. Well, I hope you'll forgive me saying so, old chap, but after six months in the trenches I thought that Ethel might provide the more convivial evening.

MARK. I see. Well, now, let me introduce Miss Prentice – Captain Philipson.

OSCAR (*eyeing her appreciatively*). How do you do?

DAPHNE. Pleased to meet you.

MARK (*meaningly*). Miss Prentice and I have been having a little dinner here – in my flat –

OSCAR. In your –

MARK (*firmly cutting him short*). Miss Prentice, incidentally, has been very kind about my flat, haven't you, Daphne?

DAPHNE. Oh yes. I think it's ever such a nice flat –

OSCAR. Splendid.

MARK. Well, anyway, as I was saying, Miss Prentice and I have been having a little dinner here – in my –

OSCAR. Yes. I've got as far as that. Go on.

MARK. And only a moment or two ago we were talking about you. I was telling her how you always stay here when you're on leave.

OSCAR. Yes, I do, don't I?

MARK. And she thought it was rather careless of you to let people like Ethel have a latchkey to my flat, but I said – or was going to say – that I didn't mind, because you and I have always been such very close friends ever since Eton – and in fact it was really you who made me take up sculpture as a profession –

OSCAR (*listening very carefully*). Ah, yes. How well I remember that.

MARK. You always had faith in me as a sculptor, didn't you, Oscar?

OSCAR. Profound.

MARK. I remember him saying to me once – I know that the name of Mark Wright is going to be famous one day. People will nudge each other in the street and say – there goes Mark Wright – the sculptor.

OSCAR (*slowly and understandingly*). And on the front of 12 Wilbraham Terrace, there'll be a little plaque saying 'Mark Wright, the sculptor, once *owned* a flat here' –

MARK. That's it. That's what you said –

OSCAR. I thought so. Well, now – may I help myself to a drink?

MARK. What? Oh yes, of course. Make this flat your own, my dear Oscar. You always do, anyhow.

OSCAR. Thank you very much.

ETHEL *emerges from the bedroom.*

Ethel, my dear. How very pleasant to see you again.

ETHEL *manages a faint and stately smile, and then extends him her cheek to kiss in the most sisterly manner.*

You've met the assembled company, haven't you?

ETHEL. The lady, yes. The gentleman is quite new to me.

OSCAR. Oh. This is Mark Wright – the famous sculptor. This is Ethel...? Ethel! Now I've got a wonderful idea. It's such a hot night – why don't you two ladies go and cool yourselves in the garden, for a moment – while I have a word with Mark –

MARK. Well – the fact is Miss Prentice and I were just on the point of leaving. Her brother has gone for a taxi –

OSCAR (*puzzled*). Her brother?

MARK. Yes. Her little brother, Sidney.

OSCAR. Well, well. We'll straighten that out later. Still, I'm afraid, Miss – Prentice, whatever Mark says, Ethel and I can't allow you both to dash off like this – on the very first night of my leave. You must at least stay and help me crack a bottle of champagne. Now, Ethel – take Miss Prentice and show her the garden by moonlight. (*To* MARK.) You don't mind Ethel showing Miss Prentice your garden by moonlight, do you, old chap?

MARK. Not a bit. I think it's a splendid idea –

DAPHNE. But do you think I should, really? Sidney'll be back any minute.

MARK. We can keep the taxi waiting. The fact is – (*Lowers his voice.*) Oscar and I have something to discuss – of a very confidential nature.

DAPHNE (*light dawning*). Oh. Oh, I see. (*Indicating* OSCAR.) He's in the same line, is he?

MARK. Much the same line.

OSCAR. What line?

DAPHNE. That's all right, Captain Philipson, Mark hasn't given anything away – I assure you.

OSCAR. Oh. I'm glad to hear it.

DAPHNE. Come on, then, Mrs er – come on. Let's see the garden.

The two girls go to the bedroom door.

ETHEL. After you.

DAPHNE *hesitates politely.*

No, I positively insist.

DAPHNE *goes out, followed by* ETHEL. OSCAR, *after a glance at* MARK, *runs out after them.*

OSCAR (*off*). Ethel. Just a word in your ear –

After a moment he reappears.

I thought I'd better inform Ethel of the change in tenancy. Now, before we go any further just exactly *what* line are you and I supposed to be in together?

MARK. The Secret Service.

OSCAR. I thought you were a sculptor.

MARK. I'm both.

OSCAR. Well, well. You've been cutting quite a dash, haven't you? You're not a famous matinee idol by any chance, or the open golf champion, or the English Nijinsky?

MARK. No. You know it all. What do you think of her?

OSCAR. Very charming. Of course she's Sylvia again. (*Indicates the bronze head.*)

MARK. Yes. Extraordinary how like, isn't it?

OSCAR. It's mad how you go stampeding through life always looking for that same face. You're not in love with her, are you?

MARK. My dear Oscar, I think she's enchanting, but only as a romantic pastime, not a serious undertaking.

OSCAR. I'm always terrified of the disaster that looms ahead for a character like you who refuses to come out of the emotional nursery. Still in love with the girl he met at seventeen. You know what you are, Mark, don't you? You're an emotional Peter Pan.

MARK. Well, what's wrong with that? I prefer to keep my emotions adolescent. They're far more enjoyable than adult ones.

OSCAR. So now after all this time as a faithful husband you've suddenly decided to become an amorist have you? An amorist, you!

MARK. Well, why not?

OSCAR. You haven't the talent, my dear fellow. Go back to being a faithful husband I implore you and leave this difficult and dangerous pastime to us trained bachelors.

MARK. Dog in the manger.

OSCAR. I scorn that. We bachelors welcome competition from married men. We so much enjoy watching them come the inevitable cropper.

MARK. There won't be any cropper, Oscar. You talk as if I were a libertine and a sensualist like yourself. I'm not. I'm a romantic, and I intend in future to give full vent to my romanticism.

OSCAR. How far has this Prentice thing gone?

MARK. No distance at all, thanks to Mum being in one of her moods –

OSCAR. Mum trouble, eh? That's bad. I'd rather Dad trouble, any day. But Mum trouble – that's very bad.

MARK. Mum is no obstacle, I shall square Mum.

OSCAR. You will square Mum? Pardon me while I snigger. Don't you realise, you poor tyro, that the process of squaring Mum is one of the most difficult, intricate, and dangerous operations in the whole field of amorism? And how, may I ask, do you propose to set about squaring Mum?

MARK. I haven't thought yet.

OSCAR. Oh, well. I suppose if you are really set on this perilous course, I shall have to give you a little tuition. What's the girl's telephone number?

MARK. I've no idea.

OSCAR. You've no idea. How typical!

There is the noise of a stone at the window.

My God! What's that?

MARK. Sidney. That's his usual way of announcing himself.

OSCAR. How old is Sidney?

MARK. About fifteen from the look of him. (*At window.*) That you, Sidney?

SIDNEY (*off*). Hi!

MARK. Yes, I thought so. Here, catch.

MARK throws down the keys to SIDNEY.

OSCAR. All right, you go and collect the girls and leave Sidney to me.

MARK. I beg your pardon.

OSCAR. I'll square Sidney.

MARK. You'll square Sidney?

OSCAR. What's the matter, what sort of a little boy is he?

MARK. Oh, you'll like him very much. He's a very clever little boy, making lots of money in munitions and –

A door is heard slamming off.

My God, there he is!

MARK goes into the bedroom as SIDNEY *enters.*

OSCAR. Hullo, my little man. Got the taxi?

SIDNEY. I've been ringing half a bleedin' hour. Don't no one ever answer a bell in this 'ouse – all gone deaf or somethin'?

OSCAR. Quite a little wag, I see. Now, Sidney, how would you like to make half a crown, eh?

SIDNEY. What for?

OSCAR. To keep your nasty little trap shut.

SIDNEY. 'Oo are you?

OSCAR. Never mind who I am. What about it, Sidney?

SIDNEY (*after a pause*). Cost you five bob.

OSCAR. Three and six, not a penny more.

SIDNEY. Five bob.

OSCAR. All right. All right – five bob it is. War profiteer!
Now go straight home and tell your Dad that you found the flat all right, but rang the bell and rang and rang and

nobody came to the door. Don't tell him any more than that and you'll be telling the truth, won't you, Sidney – which will make quite a nice change for you. Now, have you understood that?

SIDNEY. Where's my five bob?

OSCAR. There you are.

SIDNEY. Thanks. Tootaloo! (*Goes out.*)

OSCAR (*shouting after him*). And may the cigarettes you buy with it give you nicotine poisoning.

OSCAR *crosses to window.*

Hullo – cabby!

MARK *and the two girls have come in.*

ETHEL. And from that moment she was never the same again.

OSCAR (*to cab driver*). Would you wait a moment. We're just coming out.

MARK. Oh, wasn't she?

ETHEL. Never the same again.

OSCAR. Oh, Miss Prentice, did Mark tell you? He had an idea that we might all four go out together to the Savoy – and do a little dancing –

DAPHNE. Oh dear, I can't I'm afraid. You see, my family's expecting me back any minute.

OSCAR. Now, let's cope with the family trouble. What's your telephone number, Miss Prentice?

DAPHNE. You can get us on Bayswater 4302, that's the newsagents downstairs.

OSCAR. Thank you. (*Into telephone.*) Hullo… Bayswater 4302, please.

DAPHNE (*to MARK, alarmed*). Oh dear – do you think he should? I don't want to get into hot water.

MARK. I shouldn't worry too much. He's very experienced in these things, you know.

OSCAR. I may have to tell your mother a few half-truths, Miss Prentice. I hope you won't mind –

DAPHNE. Oh dear –

OSCAR (*into telephone*). Hullo... Oh, could I speak to Mrs Prentice, please? Yes, I'll wait.

DAPHNE. And anyway I couldn't go to the Savoy in a day dress, could I?

OSCAR. The dress problem I think we can cope with. Ethel has a large wardrobe, haven't you, Ethel?

ETHEL. It could be larger.

OSCAR. Yes. And I have no doubt it will be before my leave's much older. (*Into telephone.*) Is that Mrs Prentice? This is Brigadier-General Mason speaking. We've never met, I'm afraid, but a friend of mine called Mark Wright – you know – the sculptor – has brought your daughter round to my flat to a little informal party I'm giving here... Oh no, really? Oh dear... Well, then I'm afraid he's probably been ringing Wright's doorbell and hasn't been able to get a reply. It's just as well I called then, isn't it? (*Laughs easily.*) Poor little Sidney! I'm so sorry... Oh no. Surely not, Mrs Prentice? Not this minute? She's so enjoying herself. Oscar Philipson is just going to sing... Oscar Philipson, the baritone... Yes. And I'm particularly anxious for her to meet a fellow who's coming in later – you may have heard of him – Lord St Neots. He's in the Foreign Office.

MARK *starts violently.* DAPHNE *giggles.*

I think it might be useful to your daughter to meet him... Oh, that is kind of you, Mrs Prentice. Just an hour or so... Yes... Would you like to speak to your daughter?... Here she is.

DAPHNE, *fluttering, takes the telephone from him.*

DAPHNE (*into telephone*). Hullo, Mum... Yes. It's lovely here... Oh, he's ever so nice... The Brigadier-General? Oh, yes, he's ever so nice, too... Yes, Mum, and there's ever such a nice lady I've been talking to called – er – Mrs Winnington-Piggott, I think. We've become great chums... Yes, Mum. All right... cheerio, chin-chin. Nighty-night. (*She rings off and heaves a sign of relief. To* OSCAR.) Well, really, Captain – you were wonderful. You really were – I've never known Mum sound so good tempered –

OSCAR (*carelessly*). Oh, it was nothing really. Nothing at all.

He meets MARK*'s eyes, which are fixed rather crossly on him, and bows slightly.*

DAPHNE. However did you think of that silly name – Lord – what was it?

OSCAR. St Neots. I don't know. It just sprang to my lips somehow. Well, go on, girls. Jump in the taxi, get dressed up at Ethel's place, and meet us at the Savoy in half an hour –

DAPHNE. Ooh, lovely, lovely, lovely! What a thrill! Come on, Ethel.

She collects her things and dashes to the door. ETHEL *follows more impassively.*

ETHEL. What's your style, dear?

DAPHNE. Well, I don't really know, dear. It's more a question of size than of style. But I should think something simple – what have you got?

ETHEL. I'm afraid I may find it rather difficult to lay my hands on anything very simple – but let me see, now, I have got a flame-coloured spangled satin, with a rather virginal line to the neck –

Their voices fade as the front door bangs.

MARK (*explosively*). It was all nonsense what you said about my being emotionally adolescent. After seven years of married life all sorts of mysterious forces and pressures go rumbling around inside one. At any moment there might have been a catastrophic explosion. But now I've found the safety valve. A double life. It's a wonderful idea, Oscar, you know, wonderful. I wonder why more people haven't thought of it.

OSCAR. Quite a few people have. You obviously don't read the right Sunday papers.

MARK. Tell me, Oscar, how much are you paying for this flat?

OSCAR. Two-fifty a year.

MARK. Would you take five hundred furnished?

OSCAR. Certainly not.

MARK. Seven-fifty then.

OSCAR. No, don't go any higher. I'd have to accept.

MARK. Eight hundred.

OSCAR. It's fatal, you know, Mark. It'll end in the most terrible sordid tragedy. I can see the headlines now – 'Viscount's love nest raided. Incredible disclosures'. Think of your poor wife, and young Denis, Mark. Do you want Williams?

MARK. Yes.

OSCAR. That'll be another two hundred.

MARK. Done.

OSCAR. Oh dear, oh dear! My poverty but not my will consents. *Merchant of Venice*.

MARK. *Romeo and Juliet*. Of course you can stay here whenever you want.

OSCAR. Seriously, Mark, and at the risk of being a bore – it'll never work. You really can't hope to have the best of your two worlds. They'll collide and blow each other up. Mark Wright blown up would be a good thing, but I'm not keen – on seeing Mark St Neots in little pieces.

MARK. There's no reason why they should ever conflict. I intend to keep my two worlds rigidly separate.

OSCAR. You can't, you can't. Nature will take her revenge – you mark my words.

MARK. Stop talking like a character out of Thomas Hardy. What was that?

He gets up and suddenly stops on his way to the door. We now hear it too. Whistles are being distantly blown, and there is the distant sound of shouting. Suddenly a voice shouts clearly in the street outside: 'Take cover! Take cover!'

OSCAR. Zeppelins!

MARK. Oh, my God! Of all things to happen now. Denis's prayers have been answered.

OSCAR. What are you burbling about?

MARK. Look, Oscar, I'll join you at the Savoy later. I've got – to go home first.

OSCAR. Why, for heaven's sake?

MARK. I can't explain now, but Denis needs protection.

OSCAR. From the bombs, do you mean?

MARK. No. From his old imbecile of a grandfather. He'll give the poor boy hell – I must run. Just in case I get caught at home, and can't get away, explain to Daphne, will you? Tell her I'll telephone her tomorrow –

He is half out of the door when he notices OSCAR *is laughing.*

What are you laughing at?

OSCAR. Your two worlds. Rigidly separate!

MARK (*furiously*). This, let me tell you, is only an isolated incident – a purely fortuitous circumstance. It proves nothing – absolutely nothing.

OSCAR *continues laughing.*

Damn you, Oscar.

MARK *dashes out.*

Curtain.

ACT TWO

The same. Before the curtain rises, a small jazz band can be heard playing a tune of the period ('Makin' Whoopee'). The curtain rises and the band can now be determined as coming from the party in progress downstairs. The sound of voices joins the music from the band.

The year is now 1929 and the time is about 6:30 of an afternoon in late spring.

The room has undergone some changes since 1917. New curtains and covers show a feminine influence (of the jazz school) and a rearrangement of the furniture has entirely removed the rather austerely celibate air that the room once had.

At the rise of the curtain, WILLIAMS, *older by thirteen years, but dressed, as ever, in a neat blue serge suit – with a white jacket – is at the telephone. He is humming 'Makin' Whoopee'.*

WILLIAMS. Sloane 7838?... This is the Foreign Office. Could I speak to Lady Binfield, please... Oh, that is Lady Binfield speaking? Foreign Office here... I'm just ringing...

The door opens and a girl (BUBBLES) *in a very short skirt and a very boyish bob appears.*

BUBBLES (*vaguely to* WILLIAMS). Hullo?

WILLIAMS (*sharply*). Don't come in here, miss. The party's downstairs in the studio and shut the door, please! (*Holds his hand over the mouthpiece.*)

BUBBLES. Caveman!

She disappears, closing the door behind her, dispelling some of the noise.

WILLIAMS (*into telephone*). Lady Binfield?... I'm so very sorry. It was a dispatch coming in... I'm speaking for Lord

Binfield. He hadn't time to call you himself. He's had to go
very suddenly to Cheltenham on urgent business…
Cheltenham… Two or three days, I believe… Well, of
course, I wouldn't know that, being only a clerk, but I expect
it'll be something to do with the Disarmament Conference…
Yes, Lady Binfield… No, I'm afraid I can't give you his
number. It's confidential… Well, of course, I might be able to
get a message to him if it's urgent… It is… Very well, I'll
see what I can do… to ring you immediately. I see. Thank
you, Lady Binfield. Goodbye.

BUBBLES *reappears at the double doors.*

BUBBLES. Hullo! My dear, haven't we met some place
before?

WILLIAMS. I told you, miss, the party's downstairs in the
studio.

BUBBLES. I know, I just came from there. Blissful, my dear,
utterly blissful, but, my dear, no vodka.

WILLIAMS. All right, miss, if you'll go back I'll slip out and
buy you a bottle, but guests aren't really supposed to come
up here.

BUBBLES (*hugging him*). You're a gorgeous beast – (*Kisses
him.*) and I love you in that off-white affair. What's in there?
(*Pointing at bedroom door.*) Instinct tells me a bed.

WILLIAMS. Miss Patterson's in there dressing, miss. If I might
suggest –

BUBBLES. Goody. Goody. (*Flings open the bedroom door.*)
Nora, angel dear, you're giving a simply thrill-some party.
Why aren't you at it?

NORA (*off*). Go away, Bubbles, I'm in a draught.

BUBBLES. Darling, may I use your delicious bed for just a
sec? Baby has a tiny migraine and she feels she'd be better
on her back.

NORA. Isn't that the way Baby usually feels? All right, come in.

BUBBLES. Angel! (*To* WILLIAMS.) Well, goodbye, darling. It's been simply divine meeting you.

She goes into the bedroom. WILLIAMS, *with a disapproving sigh, goes to the sideboard to pick up a tray.* OSCAR *comes in. In civilian clothes he looks extremely elegant, but has put on a little weight round the girth.*

OSCAR (*extending his hand*). Hullo, Williams.

WILLIAMS. Hello, Colonel.

OSCAR. Delighted to see you again.

WILLIAMS. How are you?

OSCAR. Oh, very fit, thank you. Very fit.

WILLIAMS. You're looking very fit. You've put on a bit of weight, haven't you?

OSCAR. No. (*Pulls his stomach in instinctively.*)

WILLIAMS. I thought, perhaps, just a little round here – (*Indicates his stomach.*)

OSCAR. Nonsense. An optical illusion. Back to the light. Most deceptive. (*Puts his hat and stick on the table in the window.*) Well, where's the party?

WILLIAMS. You passed it, sir, on the way up. Didn't you hear it?

OSCAR. That bedlam downstairs?

WILLIAMS. That's right, sir, in the studio.

OSCAR. Studio?

WILLIAMS. His Lordship's taken the flat downstairs and made it into a studio, sir.

OSCAR. Good Lord. What does he want a studio for?

WILLIAMS. To sculpt in, I think. Miss Patterson's idea, of course. Very artistically minded, Miss Patterson. She's got a job all right now, sir – walking on in that new play at the Strand –

OSCAR. Tell me, Williams, what's she like?

WILLIAMS. Well, sir, I never was much of a one for the bright young people.

OSCAR. It rather depends how bright the young people are.

The sound of piano-playing mixes with the voices coming from the party.

WILLIAMS. I shouldn't think they come much brighter than Miss Patterson. Take this party of hers. Well, sir, you'd hardly credit the way they carry on downstairs. Talk about the last days of Pompeii. That reminds me. I must get back or I'll get stuck –

OSCAR. That's it, Williams. Over the top.

WILLIAMS. It *is* over the top and no perishing mistake. You coming, sir?

OSCAR. I suppose so. (*Stopping.*) Oh, before I enter the fray – it is still Mr Wright, is it, Williams?

WILLIAMS. That's right, sit. Mark Wright, 12 Wilbraham Terrace, and the Savage Club. That's what's on the cards.

OSCAR. Good Lord. Mr Wright has cards now, has he?

WILLIAMS. Oh yes, sit. Everything quite *comme il fait* –

The bedroom door is kicked open and NORA *emerges, without shoes and fiddling with the buttons of her dress. She turns her back to* OSCAR *who is standing nearer the bedroom door than* WILLIAMS, *when she speaks.*

NORA. Do me up, darling, would you? I can't reach –

OSCAR. Oh, yes. Delighted. (*Fiddles with the buttons.*)

NORA (*to* WILLIAMS). Better make some black coffee for Miss Fairweather, Williams.

WILLIAMS. Miss Fairweather, miss?

NORA. The pass-out case on my bed. (*To* OSCAR.) It's too shaming, you know, poor Bubbles – I forgot she could only drink vodka. Gin always flies straight to her head.

OSCAR (*still fiddling with the buttons*). Indeed? And where does the vodka usually fly to?

NORA. You'd be surprised. Or would you?

He fixes her dress.

Thank you, darling, you're an angel.

She goes back into the bedroom.

OSCAR. *Tiens, tiens.*

WILLIAMS. Exactly, sir.

OSCAR. Tell me, Williams, what happened to that nice Miss – what was her name?

WILLIAMS. Miss Sprigg? Same as usual, sir – got too interested – wanted to see him too often. You know the form.

OSCAR. I know the form.

WILLIAMS. She's got a hat shop now – calls herself Dahlia. His Lordship bought it for her, of course. Doing well with it, too. Quite friends they are still – but – well – you know – friends are one thing, and the other thing's the other thing, isn't it?

OSCAR. I have based my life on that belief, Williams.

MARK *comes in. He has hardly changed, except for a very slight greying of the hair.*

MARK. Williams – what are you doing gossiping up here? You're needed downstairs. Hullo, Oscar.

OSCAR. Hullo, Mark.

WILLIAMS. Sorry, my lord. I was just getting some black coffee for a Miss Fairweather.

MARK. A Miss who?

WILLIAMS. Guest that's been taken queer – in there –

MARK. Oh – and Williams, there's a man down there with grey hair and a red face and a moustache. Colonel somebody or

other. He's been shouting, 'Hullo Binfield', across the room
at me. Get him out, somehow. Spill a shaker on him, or
something –

WILLIAMS. I'll try, my lord.

MARK. And Williams – did you call my home?

WILLIAMS. Yes, my lord. Her Ladyship said you were to ring
her most particular. Something very urgent, she said.

MARK. Where exactly am I supposed to be today?

WILLIAMS. Cheltenham, sir.

MARK. I see. What's the procedure, Williams, for making a
trunk call?

WILLIAMS. Well, my lord, I suggest you get Colonel Philipson
to call the number, and say, 'Cheltenham wants you,' leave
three seconds, make a click, and then speak yourself.

OSCAR. How do we make the three pips?

WILLIAMS. I think it would be better to keep it under the three
minutes. The three pips are a bit risky. I tried it once but Her
Ladyship said there's a silly woman on the line saying
'peep'.

WILLIAMS *goes.*

MARK. Well, Oscar. How was Egypt?

OSCAR. Hot.

MARK. Are you back for good?

OSCAR. No. Only a month – damn it.

MARK. I don't know why you don't give it up. There's no
future in soldiering. We diplomats are going to see to it
there's not going to be another war.

OSCAR. My dear chap, you don't give up the Brigade of
Guards. You talk as if I were in the Army or something.

MARK. My God, you have grown a paunch, haven't you?

OSCAR. It isn't a paunch. I can pull it in. Look. (*Does so.*)

MARK. Then it comes out there.

> *He points, with some truth, to* OSCAR's *overexpanded chest.*
> *Then he walks over to* OSCAR *and extends his own rather*
> *impressively straight stomach.*

Feel that.

OSCAR (*does so*). Oh, well, of course, if you wear a corset –

MARK. A support – which has nothing whatever in common
with a corset – is a healthy and sensible garment for a man
who has reached the age of – thirty-five.

OSCAR. The age of what?

MARK. Thirty-five I said, and thirty-five I meant.

OSCAR. My poor dear old Mark, you can never hope to get
away with that. But damn it, if you're thirty-five, I'm thirty-
eight. Well, I'm only three years older than you.

MARK. Four.

OSCAR. Three. It's March now. Now even I have never tried to
get away with less than forty-two.

MARK. Yes. I think that's very wise of you. (*Into telephone.*)
Hullo, I want Sloane 7838 please. (*To* OSCAR.) Now if
that's plainly understood, perhaps you'll be kind enough to
give your famous imitation of Cheltenham on the
telephone.

> OSCAR *reluctantly goes to the telephone.*

OSCAR. You thirty-five – with a hulking great son on the verge
of being a diplomat.

MARK. He's not hulking and he's got a good four years to go
yet before he's a diplomat. That's to say if he gets in.

OSCAR (*indicating telephone*). Engaged.

MARK. Damn it. Who on earth is she talking to?

OSCAR. Why shouldn't Denis get in? He's got brains, that boy. You mustn't underestimate my godson.

MARK. He's a damn little slacker. He's been at this place in Tours for three months and he can't even write a line of a letter in reasonably correct French. Keeps complaining that the daughter of the house has fallen in love with him.

OSCAR. I don't understand what he has to complain about in that.

MARK. I'm sure you don't. But Denis, I am happy to tell you, has inherited his father's romantic nature.

OSCAR. Don't say he's acquired a Sylvia too, since I've been away.

MARK. A rather deplorable one, I'm afraid. Ursula Culpepper.

OSCAR. Ursula Culpepper? Oh, my God!

MARK. You know her? Off the stage, I mean –

OSCAR. It's hard not to know her, isn't it? His Uncle Oscar will have to have a very severe word with him. Oh dear, oh dear! What do these children see in her?

MARK. Glamour, I suppose. She uses a lot of words very loudly that they've only previously read chalked on walls.

OSCAR. An unsuitable Sylvia – I grant you.

MARK. Exactly. I've put my foot down pretty hard, I may say I had to, of course. He won't see her again.

OSCAR. Good. Oh, by the way, Mark – congratulations on your new appointment.

MARK. Thanks. How did you hear?

OSCAR. It was in *The Londoner's Diary*. Didn't you read it?

MARK. No. What did it say?

OSCAR. Oh, something about Lord Binfield being our new Minister in La Paz.

MARK. Oh. Nothing else?

OSCAR. No. I don't think there was anything else.

MARK (*nastily*). Oh, wasn't there? Well, then, perhaps this will refresh your memory. (*Takes a newspaper cutting from his pocket. Reading.*) 'The Earl of Binfield, a well-known and popular figure in Brussels, where he has been our Counsellor of Embassy since 1926 – '

OSCAR. You said you hadn't read it –

MARK. Well, I have! '... is today to be congratulated on a new appointment fitting to his brilliant attainments.'

OSCAR (*sulkily*). All right, all right, I remember.

MARK. How does it go on?

OSCAR. Oh, something about your being thin –

MARK (*reading*). 'Slim. Slim, handsome, and witty, Lord Binfield, who inherited the title from his father in 1923 – '

OSCAR. Yes, yes. I'll try that number again. (*Goes to the telephone.*) Get me Sloane 7838 please. (*To MARK.*) Friend of yours, this Londoner fellow, I presume?

MARK. Never met the man in my life. (*Puts the cutting away.*)

OSCAR. They said something like that about me once.

MARK. What did they say?

OSCAR. Oh – something about being one of the best-looking officers in the Brigade of Guards – you know – something rather embarrassing like that. (*Hastily, into telephone.*) Oh, is that – I mean are you – er – (*Prompted by MARK.*) Sloane 7838... You are. Splendid. Br – er – Cheltenham – that's it – Cheltenham wants you... hold on.

MARK, *after glaring at* OSCAR, *takes the telephone.*

(*Whispering frantically.*) Click! Click!

MARK (*whispering back*). Click off. (*After a pause, into telephone.*) Hullo? Hullo, darling... Can you hear me all right?... Yes, I can hear you. They tell me you were trying to get hold of me. Oh, my God... is he there? Well, where is he?... Well, why did you let him?... Game of squash, I don't think. More likely drinking in a Bloomsbury bar, with Ursula Culpepper and her crowd of degenerates.

OSCAR. Denis?

MARK (*to* OSCAR). Yes. (*Into telephone.*) Is he deigning to come back to dinner?... You don't think so. That's charming... Sorry for him? Well, I can assure you you're going to be a good deal sorrier for him when I get through with him... Well, what do you expect me to do? Pat him on the back and say, 'Well done, little man. Ruin your career. I'm proud of you'? Well, it's going to be difficult for me, but I shall come up first thing tomorrow morning – even if it's – only for a few hours – No. I can't tonight... No. Utterly impossible. You can tell him from me he's not going to enjoy the interview, and he'd better buy his ticket back to Tours first thing in the morning... Goodbye... 'Victorian'? Really, what a ridiculous – Hullo, hullo.

He takes the telephone from his ear and replaces it slowly. The sound of the party is heard.

Victorian. Me?

OSCAR. At thirty-five.

MARK. Shut up. (*Morosely.*) The damn little fool!

OSCAR. Done a bunk?

MARK. Doesn't like it over there. Decided he's going to be an actor.

OSCAR. Oh. Can he act?

MARK. No, of course not.

OSCAR. How do you know?

MARK. I've seen him.

OSCAR. What as?

MARK. Shylock.

OSCAR. What was he like?

MARK. Unspeakable.

OSCAR. Well, perhaps he wasn't very well cast.

MARK (*aggressively*). Are *you* taking his side against me too?

OSCAR (*hastily*). No, no. It's just that – well, after all, there are always two sides to every question, aren't there?

MARK. Who the hell says so?

OSCAR (*pacifically*). No one says so, old chap. It's just that it's a sort of – generally accepted theory –

MARK. Well, it's a damn silly theory. My God, the way they allow these boys to act in these plays at school is a positive scandal. Filling their heads with all sorts of dangerous subversive ideas –

OSCAR (*reminiscently*). Come to think of it, I was rather good as Lady Macbeth.

MARK (*viciously*). You were ghastly as Lady Macbeth. You were absolutely excruciating as Lady Macbeth.

OSCAR (*with dignity*). The *Etonian* said I took my part with spirit and courage –

MARK. The *Etonian* must have been out of its mind.

The door opens and NORA *emerges, dressed very daringly for the party. The strains of 'Dance Little Lady' can be heard from downstairs.*

NORA. Oh, hullo, darlings.

MARK. Oh, hullo, darling. I don't think you've met Oscar Philipson, have you? He's one of my very oldest and dearest friends –

NORA. No. How do you do?

OSCAR. As a matter of fact, we met a moment ago.

NORA. Did we?

OSCAR. I was the one who did you up – do you remember?

NORA. Oh, my God, yes. A skilful and practised hand, I thought, too –

OSCAR. Oh, did you? That's very good of you.

NORA. Darling, it's too wonderful to meet you at last. I've heard so much about you from Mark.

OSCAR. Oh, you mustn't believe all that Mark says, you know.

NORA. My God, no. You're so right. I mean, from what he said, I thought you'd be quite old and staid and ordinary and, my God, look at you, a positive dreamboat, my dear –

OSCAR (*delighted*). A 'dreamboat'? Oh, do you really think so –

NORA. An absolute gondola, my dear. But what, I'm here to ask, are we all doing up here? I mean, isn't there a party on somewhere, or isn't there?

MARK. Oh, yes. It's still there, I think.

NORA. My God, without a host or hostess? It's too shaming for words. Why have you deserted your post, you wicked man?

MARK. Only under fire, my dear. There's a terrible man down there I've taken an acute dislike to –

NORA. Oh, my dear, I'm sure there are a hundred terrible men down there I'm going to take a positive, burning hatred to, but really that couldn't be less here or there, now, could it? Or could it? My darlings, let's fly to our deadly social duties this instant –

MARK. No, I'm not going down again until that Colonel's gone. Oscar, run down, would you, and see if he's still there?

OSCAR. Well, what does he look like?

MARK. Red-faced, grey hair, grey moustache, loud voice. You can't mistake him. He's the only one there even remotely the type.

OSCAR (*at the door*). But – dash it all – I won't know anyone down there.

MARK. Yah! Windy!

OSCAR (*considering him*). Witty. Slim, handsome, and witty. *The Londoner*!

He makes a face and departs.

NORA. What did he mean?

MARK. Some obscure joke. (*Kisses her.*) How are you? I haven't seen you for nearly three whole days.

NORA. Darling – devastated with mad expectancy for this wonderful weekend. (*Showing her dress.*) You haven't said yet?

MARK. Oh, is that the new get-up?

She shows it off by walking up and down.

Oh yes. It's exquisite.

NORA. Quite an exquisite price too, darling. Does that matter?

He looks at her, smiling.

Or does it?

MARK (*embracing her*). It doesn't.

NORA. Mr Wright, I adore you. (*Holds his hands.*) Darling, you really must be madly rich –

MARK. Not *madly* rich.

NORA. But where do you get it all from, darling? Surely not out of sculpting?

MARK. Oh, well. There's the other work, too, you know.

NORA. The Secret Service? But they pay you nothing in that – my dear – a positive pittance – I know. Look at Flossie Philips.

MARK. Flossie Philips?

NORA. Darling, you must know Flossie. She's terribly important in your little affair. X101 or some such madly gay number, and she has trouble even to get her bus fares paid. So where, I'd like to know, darling, does all this gorgeous money, which I frankly dote on, come from?

MARK. Does it matter?

NORA. No. Not awfully. Madly mysterious you are, aren't you? But I'll find out, don't worry. Darling, what's all this lunacy about going to La Paz or somewhere?

MARK. Well, it's true, I'm afraid.

NORA. But why La Paz, for God's sake?

MARK. We're not allowed to choose where we're sent.

NORA. But, darling, La Paz! My God, it's the other end of the earth. Now Brussels wasn't so bad – you could get over for weekends. But La Paz. You can't go to La Paz.

MARK (*tenderly*). Can't I?

NORA. No. Tell them you won't go. My God, there's far more Secret Service to be done in London than in La Paz. Tell them to keep you in London.

MARK. I've told them. They won't.

NORA. Then tell them to go to hell.

MARK. I've thought of that too.

NORA. Have you? On the level?

MARK. On the level.

NORA. Are you going to?

MARK. I don't know. It's a very big decision.

NORA. Can I help you to make it?

MARK. Yes.

NORA. How?

MARK. By looking at me as you are now.

NORA. Like Sylvia, you mean?

MARK. No. Not like Sylvia. Like Nora.

Pause.

NORA. You realise I must go down to my party, don't you?

MARK. Yes. But I also realise that later tonight you're going to look at me in the same way as you're doing now.

After a pause he turns her to the door.

NORA (*at the door*). Darling – I've got a wonderful idea. Why on earth didn't I think of it before –

MARK. What?

NORA. I'll get Flossie Philips to fix it.

MARK (*vehemently*). No, don't, for heaven's sake!

NORA. But, darling, one word from Flossie and you're in London for years –

MARK. Darling, one word from Flossie and I'm in Queer Street for life. No, Nora. Thank you very much, but we're really not supposed to talk about these things, and I can get into very serious trouble if you mention it. Be an angel. Not a word.

NORA. On one condition.

MARK. What?

NORA. You know.

Pause.

MARK. Then give me a truthful answer to a sincere question.

NORA. Right.

MARK. If I did that, would you stay with me for life?

Pause.

NORA. Yes.

MARK. Thank you. See you in a minute.

NORA opens the door and lets in the sound of the party.

NORA (*listening*). My God, it sounds as dead as a doorknob. I'd better get Babs to do her fan dance – if she's still vertical. Don't be long, darling.

She disappears. Almost simultaneously, BUBBLES, tousled and shoeless, appears in the bedroom door, staring at MARK through half-closed eyes.

BUBBLES. Has Ponsonby brought the vodka yet?

MARK (*politely*). Who is Ponsonby? And what vodka is he bringing?

BUBBLES. My good man – I am not here to bandy words with a complete stranger –

MARK. What are you here for?

BUBBLES. I've no idea. (*Disappears into the bedroom again and closes the door.*)

OSCAR darts in through the hall door.

OSCAR (*in alarm*). My God, Mark – you know that Colonel of yours?

MARK. Yes?

OSCAR. I'm flying for my life.

MARK. Why?

OSCAR. Husband trouble.

MARK. Serves you right. You shouldn't have husband trouble at all. It's utterly against the rules.

OSCAR. The game I play – which is entirely of my own invention – has, happily – no rules of any kind. May I make myself a cocktail?

MARK. Why?

OSCAR. Well, I'm not going to get one downstairs, it seems.

MARK. Yes. All right. Everything's there. Make one for me too.

OSCAR (*at the sideboard*). Luckily he's never seen me – this Colonel Wilberforce, but some idiot told him I was at the party, and now he's roaring across the room about having a word or two to say to this young rotter Philipson.

MARK. 'Young rotter'? Oh, well, of course, you were saying he'd never seen you.

OSCAR. And you tell me my humour is fourth form. There's no ice.

MARK. Of course there's no ice.

OSCAR. I used to keep it in a sort of vacuum thingammajig. What's happened to it?

MARK. You took it.

OSCAR. So I did. Well, as I was saying, this mutual menace of ours, this Colonel Wilberforce, has an entirely misguided notion that I once took certain liberties with Mrs Wilberforce in a taxi going from the Pyramids to the Cairo Opera House. (*Tries the cocktail.*) This tastes rather good. Do you know, I think it's better without ice.

MARK. How misguided was the Colonel's notion?

OSCAR. Oh, entirely. It wasn't in a taxi at all.

MARK. On a camel?

OSCAR. Fourth form. Fourth form. It was in a beautiful moonlit garden, and I didn't take liberties. I was accorded them.

MARK. God, what have you put in this thing? (*Indicates his cocktail, which he has just sipped.*)

OSCAR. Ordinary gin and French. It's that little touch of lemon that makes the difference.

MARK. It's got a sort of sickly taste – like a decaying turnip.

OSCAR. Nonsense. It's delicious.

He drinks his down. MARK puts his aside.

MARK. Oscar – I've got something very serious to tell you. Can I have your whole attention, please?

OSCAR *nods. There is a pause.*

What do you think of her?

OSCAR. Her? Oh, charming, charming – of course, she's Sylvia, version 1929 – bang up to date.

MARK. Sylvia doesn't come into it this time.

OSCAR. Of course she does. This girl is the living image –

MARK. I know. It makes no difference. I'm not in love with an image. I'm in love with Nora Patterson.

OSCAR. I knew this would happen one day. You can't say I haven't warned you. Oh, Lord – I suppose I shall have to give evidence.

MARK. Evidence? Where?

OSCAR (*crossing to sideboard for another drink*). At the divorce.

MARK. Divorce? Whose divorce?

OSCAR. Your divorce of course.

MARK. Don't be so infernally melodramatic. Who's talking about divorce?

OSCAR. You said you were in love with –

MARK. Well, so I am. All I'm trying to tell you is I'm sufficiently in love with her to give up the Diplomatic.

Pause.

OSCAR. *Tiens, tiens.*

MARK. What did you say?

OSCAR. I said, *tiens, tiens*. It's a French expression meaning 'hold, hold'.

MARK. Have you any other comment?

OSCAR. Only that sitting on this very sofa – many years ago –
I warned you of this very disaster – I remember it perfectly.
Your two worlds, I said, will collide, and blow each other up.
Mark Wright blown up, I said, will be a good thing. But
Mark Binfield blown up, I said – will be a catast –
catastrophe. Do you know – I think I did put something
rather funny in this. (*Indicates his cocktail.*)

MARK (*after sipping his own glass*). You know what you've
done, don't you. You've put brandy in instead of vermouth.

OSCAR. Ridiculous. I couldn't have – (*Goes to the drink
sideboard.*) There's the gin. And there's the – (*Sniffs the
second decanter. Furiously.*) Well, of all the idiotic things to
do – to go and put brandy in the vermouth decanter.

MARK. That's the brandy decanter. There's no such thing as a
vermouth decanter.

OSCAR. Certainly there's such a thing as a vermouth decanter.
This is the vermouth decanter. I always kept vermouth in this
decanter –

MARK. Well, I keep brandy in it.

OSCAR. You realise what you've done, don't you? Quite apart
from rendering me insensible hours before my normal time,
you've very probably given me another of my livers. (*Bad
temperedly.*) What were we talking about?

MARK. Me – giving up the Diplomatic.

OSCAR. Oh yes. Catastrophe. (*Surprised.*) I said it all right that
time.

MARK. Nonsense.

OSCAR (*crossly*). I did say it all right –

MARK. I mean, it's nonsense to sit there just burbling
'catastrophe'.

OSCAR (*darkly*). You'll see, my boy. You'll see. Oh, and I have
one further comment to make. A brief comment but one of
extraordinary penetrative – penetrativeness –

MARK. Try penetration.

OSCAR. I've said penetrativeness now.

MARK. Make the comment.

OSCAR. Denis.

MARK. That's idiotic. Denis is eighteen. He can't possibly know his own mind, while I know exactly what I'm doing –

OSCAR. The difference, in fact, between suicide while of unsound mind and *felo de se*. Do you know that's rather good? I wish someone could have heard that.

MARK. I heard it, and thought it damn silly. Besides, Denis thinks he's going to be an actor –

OSCAR. What do you think you're going to be?

MARK. Myself. No more than that. I'll sculpt a bit more, perhaps – write a little – read all the books I ought to have read –

OSCAR. You can do all that in La Paz.

MARK. Yes, but why La Paz, for heaven's sake? Why should I, in the prime of life –

OSCAR. Slim, handsome, and witty –

MARK. Shut up. Why should I incarcerate myself in a place like La Paz – probably for years and years – exiled, forgotten, humiliated, ignored – in some moth-eaten little South American dust heap?

OSCAR. It's a delightful city, La Paz.

MARK. Have you been there?

OSCAR. I've had a postcard.

MARK. Minister in La Paz! I tell you, Oscar, if I give in now, I give in to old age, and dullness and respectability and drab security and all the things I've been trying to run away from in the last thirteen years – ever since I invented Mark Wright. Very well – the two worlds *have* collided – who cares? Better

Binfield go under than Wright. Binfield is nothing – there are millions like him – respectable, domesticated, frustrated bores, half-dead without knowing it. But Wright is alive – he has a great capacity for living – and life should be lived in the full tide – not snoozed away in stagnant backwaters. I tell you, Oscar, I have reached my turning point – the moment that comes to a man once and only once in his lifetime – when he has to make a Napoleonic decision – a decision that is going to make or mar him for the rest of his time on earth. Well, I've made mine. I'm resigning from the Service tomorrow.

OSCAR *is staring at him fixedly.*

Well?

OSCAR. Extraordinary the way your eyebrows move about when you get excited.

MARK. Any further comment?

OSCAR. Yes.

MARK. What?

OSCAR. Disaster. Utter cata – disaster –

WILLIAMS *comes in with a tray on which is a coffee pot, a bottle, and a cup.*

MARK. Has that damn Colonel gone yet?

WILLIAMS. No, my lord. I spilled a tomato juice on him, like you said, but he hardly seemed to notice it. (*Goes into the bedroom.*)

MARK. What on earth can we do to get rid of him?

After a second's pause the same idea occurs to them simultaneously. The both turn and look at the shaker. They get up and go to the sideboard.

Can you remember the exact formula?

OSCAR. Of course. A perfectly ordinary dry Martini, my dear chap. (*Mixes a cocktail, using the same decanters as before.*)

Two parts gin – one part vermouth – a touch more vermouth, I think, don't you – don't let's be stingy – and then just a dash of lemon, which brings the whole thing to glorious life. There we are. (*Sips it.*) Yes. That is the veritable brew. The Philipson patent husband-remover or Binfield-shouter slayer.

WILLIAMS *emerges from the bedroom.* MARK *takes the shaker from* OSCAR *and hands it to* WILLIAMS.

MARK. Ah, Williams, this is for Colonel Wilberforce only. Only, understand.

WILLIAMS. Yes, my lord.

MARK. But be careful. Don't spill it, or we'll have a hole in the floor.

OSCAR. What was it you just took into the bedroom, Williams?

WILLIAMS. Black coffee – and vodka – sir, for one of the guests.

OSCAR. Oh. What sex is the guest?

WILLIAMS. Female, sir.

OSCAR. Below the age of thirty?

WILLIAMS. Yes, sir.

OSCAR. What is her name?

WILLIAMS. Oh! I heard Miss Patterson call her Bubbles.

OSCAR. Bubbles. Bring another cup, would you?

He goes into the bedroom.

MARK. The second this Colonel Wilberforce falls in a stupor, bundle him into a taxi – and let me know –

WILLIAMS. Yes, my lord.

NORA *comes in.*

NORA. Darling, really – you *are* too naughty. They're all screaming for you downstairs.

MARK. I can't come down just yet, darling. I really can't. But, with Williams's help, I have the highest hopes of being down in a very few minutes now – all right, Williams. Thank you.

He nods to WILLIAMS, *who goes out.*

NORA. Well, don't leave it too long, darling, or they'll all begin to believe Mark Wright doesn't exist.

MARK. Mark Wright does exist. In fact, Mark Wright has just made a very momentous decision.

NORA. No La Paz?

MARK. No La Paz.

NORA. Thank you. I can't say more. Just thank you. I must go back. Darling, there's someone actually aching to meet you. I was showing him some of your work and he said he recognised it.

MARK (*pleased*). Oh. Who was that?

NORA. I can't remember his name. Viscount someone or other. He came with Ursula Culpepper. I'll send him up.

MARK (*gently*). Darling – two things. First, I told you I didn't want Ursula Culpepper at this party – I detest and deplore the woman –

NORA. You can't keep her out, darling. Besides, she *is* my leading lady – after all. I'm so sorry. What's the second thing?

MARK. Well, it's a very tiny little snob point, but you did ask me once to put you right on these things, didn't you?

NORA. Yes, darling –

MARK. Well, one doesn't talk about 'Viscount So-and-so' – one says 'Lord' – (*An appalling thought strikes him. Stops as if shot.*) Viscount who, did you say?

NORA. St Something.

MARK (*in agony*). With Ursula Culpepper?

NORA. Yes.

MARK. How old?

NORA. Oh. Eighteen – nineteen.

MARK. Yes. I see. (*Looks wildly round the room as if meditating diving through the window.*) Darling – would you think it awfully odd of me if I went out for a little stroll?

NORA. But darling, my party.

MARK. Yes, I know, darling. But sometimes I get the most terrible, terrible claustrophobia at parties.

The words freeze on his lips as DENIS *appears.*

NORA. This is the boy I was telling you about, dear. (*To* DENIS.) Darling, what was that name again?

DENIS. St Neots.

NORA. That's right. Viscount – sorry – Lord St Neots – Mr Wright. I'll leave you two together. (*To* MARK.) Goodbye, my precious. (*Kisses him on the cheek.*) Now don't be too long. I mean, it's really too blush-making to give a party just to show off one's gorgeous, glamorous lover, and then he just doesn't put in an appearance at all.

She goes out. There is an endless pause after she has gone.

MARK (*at length*). These young girls nowadays have a rather exaggerated way of expressing themselves sometimes.

DENIS. Yes. I know.

MARK. It's what they call being modern, I suppose.

DENIS. I suppose so. (*Pause.*) Very old-fashioned, really, isn't it?

MARK. Yes, I suppose it is. (*Pause.*) You're looking very brown.

DENIS. I've been sunbathing a lot.

MARK. Yes. Of course. (*Pause.*) Appearances, you know, Denis, can often be very deceptive.

DENIS. Yes. I know.

MARK. I only say that because I don't want you to jump to any hasty or rash conclusions.

DENIS. No, Father, I won't.

MARK. I don't know whether you know – as a matter of fact I don't think you do – that for some time past now I have been engaged on a little – undercover work for the Government. I won't tell you any more than that – but you can probably guess what I'm hinting at.

DENIS. Yes, I think I can.

MARK. Good. Good. Oh, by the way, I'd rather you didn't give my real name away here if you can avoid it.

DENIS. Of course I won't.

MARK. Miss Patterson and I, of course, are old friends – very old friends.

DENIS. Yes. I rather gather so –

MARK. But even she doesn't know my real identity –

OSCAR appears at the bedroom door, on the arm of BUBBLES.

OSCAR. A nymph! I have found myself a nymph. And vodka, let me tell you, is the tipple of the world.

He comes face to face with the grave-faced DENIS.

Tiens, tiens.

DENIS. Hullo, Uncle Oscar.

Pause.

OSCAR (*heartily*). Hullo, Denis. You're looking very brown.

MARK. He's been sunbathing.

OSCAR. Oh yes, of course. That would account for it. Well, well, well, well, well. (*After a pause.*) Well, well, well.

BUBBLES (*to* OSCAR). My God, darling – stop saying 'well', it's too shamingly repetitious, and go on with that lovely tickling thing you were doing to the back of my neck –

OSCAR. Er – Miss Fairweather – I wonder if you'd mind awfully going back to bed for a moment. (*Pushes her towards the door.*)

BUBBLES. Well, give me my vodka – (*Takes it, and kisses him on the cheek.*) Baby's not going to be left entirely on her own. (*At the door.*) I'll be waiting, you gorgeous beast. I'll be waiting – (*Goes.*)

OSCAR. Extraordinary the high spirits of these youngsters, isn't it?

MARK. Yes, it is, isn't it?

OSCAR. Extraordinary. (*Heartily again.*) Well, Denis – quite a surprise bumping into you like this.

DENIS. Yes, I know.

OSCAR (*carefully*). Your father's probably told you about how I happened to see him at the Club, and how I said I wanted him to come along to a party that a chap called Wright was giving, because I thought it might amuse him, you know, and of course this girl Nora Patterson is quite an old friend of mine – and your father hadn't even met her, so I thought –

He stops, noticing the expression on MARK*'s face.*

Isn't that what he told you?

DENIS. No. Not exactly.

OSCAR (*aggrieved*). Well, I can't for the life of me think why not.

MARK. Your Uncle Oscar isn't quite accountable for his actions at the moment, you know, Denis. He had a silly accident with a cocktail he was mixing, and put brandy in instead of vermouth. Imagine.

DENIS. Horrible, I should think. And then, of course, with vodka on top – look, Father – I'm awfully sorry about this. I hope you don't think I've done it on purpose or anything – but I was downstairs and Miss Patterson was showing me some sculpture and, of course, I recognised some of it, so I thought I'd better meet this chap Wright, because I thought perhaps some blighter was pinching your work or something.

MARK. That's all right, my dear boy. That's perfectly all right. I quite understand.

DENIS. Of course it was idiotic of me, because I should have realised the situation at once.

MARK. Oh? Why should you?

DENIS. Well, as soon as I saw Miss Patterson –

MARK. I don't quite follow.

DENIS. Well, of course, she's the living image of Sylvia, isn't she?

MARK. Sylvia?

DENIS. That face you're always sculpting. The one you were in love with when you were seventeen –

MARK. Oh. How did you know that?

DENIS. You told me about her.

MARK. I never told you I was in love with her –

DENIS. Oh well, Father, that was easy to guess, wasn't it?

MARK. Was it? I didn't know.

DENIS. It's funny, you know. I imagine an awful lot of people go through life in love with the same face.

MARK. Yes. I imagine they do.

DENIS. It's arrested development, really, isn't it?

MARK. Is it?

DENIS. A sort of narcissism, I think.

MARK. Narcissism?

DENIS. Well, you know – what you're really in love with is your vanished youth.

OSCAR *makes a slight sound.*

MARK (*savagely to* OSCAR). Did you say anything?

OSCAR. No, no. Just a sneeze – that's all.

DENIS. You see, it's really yourself at seventeen that you love.

MARK. Do I?

DENIS. Yes. (*Smiling cheerfully.*) Oh, it's nothing at all to worry about, Father.

MARK. I'm delighted to hear it.

DENIS. I mean – you don't need to go to a psychoanalyst or anything.

MARK. That's good. Psychoanalysts are so expensive, aren't they?

DENIS. Well, as a matter of fact, Father, I do happen to know a very good one in Wigmore Street who'd do you at a reduced rate – if you really wanted to go, that's to say – but I honestly don't think it's necessary. I mean, arrested development's awfully common, really. Practically everyone has it, in one form or another –

MARK. Uncle Oscar, for instance?

DENIS. Oh yes. Of course. That's terribly obvious, isn't it?

OSCAR. Is it?

DENIS. Tickling girls on the back of – the neck, and all that. It's really children's games, isn't it – I mean, from a strictly Freudian point.

Pause.

OSCAR. Tell me, Denis. What is the address of this man in Wigmore Street?

DENIS. I haven't got it on me. But I'm sure there's nothing to worry about, Father. This looking for Sylvia is really quite harmless. Quite harmless. Well, now, look. I know you'd rather I didn't stay, and I'd like to leave if I could – because I've promised to take Ursula to dinner –

MARK. You mean Ursula Culpepper?

DENIS. Yes.

There is a pause. Then MARK *gathers himself for assault.*

MARK. Ah! Now I thought I had expressly forbidden you ever to see that woman again?

OSCAR (*murmuring*). My front is being pierced, my flanks are being turned, I attack. Marshal Foch.

MARK (*after glaring at* OSCAR). Is that, or is that not so, Denis?

DENIS. Yes, Father. But I never promised and I'm afraid I didn't accept your judgement in this case.

MARK. Oh? You didn't? Well, you'd better accept it now. I won't have my son consorting with one of the most notorious women in London.

DENIS. She can't help being notorious, Father. She's such a famous actress. Wonderful actress, too. Have you ever seen her?

MARK. No. I am happy to say, not.

DENIS. I'm surprised. She's starring in the same play that Miss Patterson is a super in –

Pause.

OSCAR. Of course that flank was badly exposed – invited counter-attack –

MARK (*after another glance at* OSCAR). A woman with the mind and the vocabulary of a streetwalker –

DENIS. Yes, I know, Father. It's awfully boring, that outspokenness. I often tell her so. It's what we were saying a moment ago about Miss Patterson, isn't it?

OSCAR. Oh dear. Clean through the centre now.

MARK. Oscar, I trust I shall not have to ask you to leave the room.

OSCAR. I'm sorry. It's the vodka –

MARK (*to* DENIS). Leaving the subject of Ursula Culpepper for the moment only – Denis – may I ask you for an explanation of your extraordinary conduct in leaving Tours at a moment's notice, and flying to London?

DENIS. I'm sorry, Father, but I couldn't stick it there another second. After all I'd been there three months –

MARK. And how much French have you learnt in those three months, may I ask? *Dites-moi quelque chose en francais –*

DENIS. *Que voulez-vous que je vous dis?*

MARK (*triumphantly*). *Dise. Que je vous dise.* Subjunctive. And your accent is abominable.

OSCAR. Ah. An advance. A minor one – perhaps – but still an advance –

MARK (*furiously*). Oscar – will you keep quiet?

DENIS. Anyway, Father, there's no real point in my learning French, is there, because I've decided to become an actor.

MARK. Oh, you have, have you? You've decided to become an actor?

NORA *comes in.*

NORA. Darling, I'm just going to put on that new hat you gave me, to show Babs. (*Crosses to the bedroom door.*) What *is* going on up here?

MARK. Nothing, my dear. Nothing.

NORA. Darling, if you don't come down in a minute I think I'll get cross. Except that I couldn't really get cross with you, today, could I, after your being such a sweetie and giving up that horrid, horrid La Paz for me –

MARK. Yes, well, we'll talk about all that later.

She goes into the bedroom.

DENIS (*reproachfully*). Oh, Father! You're not giving up the Diplomatic, are you?

Pause.

OSCAR (*to* MARK). I think, my dear chap – there's nothing for it but to prepare for an eventual evacuation –

MARK. Oscar. Leave the room.

OSCAR. I was on the point of doing so. The whole scene is far too painful for me.

COLONEL WILBERFORCE's *jovial head appears at the door.* OSCAR *flies to a corner of the room and examines a picture.*

WILBERFORCE. Ah, Binfield. So that's where you've been hiding yourself, is it? Can't say I blame you. Terrible party, isn't it?

MARK. You're not enjoying it, Colonel?

WILBERFORCE. Hating it, my dear fellow. Positively hating it. Of course, I'd never have come if it hadn't been for my wife. She was on the stage, you know. (*Seeing* DENIS.) Oh, isn't this your boy?

MARK. Yes.

WILBERFORCE. I thought so. Saw you bat at Lord's, young fellow. Shouldn't have got out that way. Shocking stroke. Yes, my wife was in that show *Topsy-Turvy*. Expect you saw it. She was the one who came out at the end and said, 'So you were really Lord Percy all along?' Do you remember?

MARK. Yes, of course.

WILBERFORCE. Good. You heard her all right, did you?

MARK. As clear as a bell.

WILBERFORCE. I only ask because some friends of mine said they had difficulty in catching the words. Of course I couldn't really judge because, you see, I knew the part.

MARK. No. I see. Exactly –

OSCAR *is examining the picture with great apparent interest.* WILBERFORCE *looks at him with faint suspicion.*

WILBERFORCE. Tell me, does anyone here know a terrible bounder by the name of Philipson?

He says it to OSCAR *who shakes his head vaguely.*

I hear he's at this party. I'm extremely anxious to have a word with the blighter –

After a pregnant pause, DENIS *steps forward.*

DENIS. Er – may I introduce – Brigadier Mason – er – Colonel –

WILBERFORCE. Wilberforce. How do you do? You're very young to be a Brigadier.

OSCAR. So many people tell me –

There is the sound of a woman singing raucously, loudly, and drunkenly in the street.

WILBERFORCE. Oh. Excuse me a second. I think that's my wife – (*Crossing to window.*) Yes, it is. Astonishing thing. Never drinks at all, you know. All she ever does at a party is to take an occasional sip from my glass.

MARK. Indeed, Colonel? Is that all she ever does? Just take an occasional sip from your glass?

WILBERFORCE. Yes. That's all. Can't understand it at all – (*Out of window to his invisible wife.*) Hullo, darling. Yoo-hoo!

A woman's voice is heard in response.

Look – you – there – Williams, isn't it?

WILLIAMS (*off*). Okay, sir.

WILBERFORCE. Now just you get hold of her.

Her voice is heard in protest.

Don't let go of her, man. Get her into that taxi.

There is the noise of a taxi door slamming, then silence.

Safely stowed, as they say in the play. Williams did it on his own – capital fellow, that. Goodbye, young feller. Keep a straighter bat next time. Goodbye, Brigadier. Goodbye, Binfield. Nice seeing you again.

NORA *emerges from the bedroom.*

Ah, our hostess. Just saying goodbye –

NORA. Oh. Are you leaving so soon?

WILBERFORCE. Yes. Slight accident to Betty. Can't fathom it. Can't fathom it at all. Goodbye. Charming party. Afraid I never had a chance to meet our host. Say goodbye to him for me, would you?

NORA (*indicating* MARK) Well, you can do it yourself, can't you?

WILBERFORCE. What! Binfield! Binfield the host! That's good, isn't it, old chap? Well, goodbye, everyone. Oh, Binfield, congratulations on being made Minister in La Paz, by the way. Splendid appointment. Splendid. Goodbye. (*Goes, leaving a heavy silence behind him.*)

NORA. Darling, you'll forgive me for being inquisitive, won't you?

There is a pause. Then MARK *clears his throat resignedly.*

MARK. Nora, I realise perfectly that what I am going to tell you may seem not unlike the plot of *Topsy-Turvy*, but I must inform you that I am not Mr Wright, but Lord Binfield; and that this is my son, Denis.

NORA (*seizing the salient point*). Your son? (*Looks at* DENIS *and then at* MARK.) Oh, darling. I mean you couldn't have really – could you?

MARK. No. My age, too, I have lied about. I am not thirty-five, but forty-four.

NORA. Darling! Three one can forgive. Nine is really going too far. Well, it's all too wildly exciting and improbable – just like *life*, my darlings – but we really haven't time to discuss it all now. I'm going back to the party. (*Goes to the door.*) Oh, by the way – in case anybody's even remotely interested – I am actually the rightful Princess Amalia of Bottleburg and Bubbles Fairweather is my mother – the Grand Duchess –

She goes out. There is a long pause.

OSCAR (*at length*). *Tiens, tiens.*

MARK *sits heavily, and rests his head in his hands.*

(*Again.*) *Tiens, tiens.*

DENIS *goes up to* MARK's *chair.* MARK *looks up at him, glaring.*

DENIS. Father, may I say something?

MARK *looks at him in silence.*

I know it's none of my business – but really, you know, I do think you're making rather a mistake chucking the Diplomatic. (*Very sincerely.*) I know exactly how you feel and I do sympathise with you – really I do. But you've had such a brilliant career up to now – haven't you – I do think it'd be an awful waste to throw it all away now.

MARK *still makes no reply. He seems rather moved.*

... Could we have dinner together, Father?

MARK. I understood you were dining with Ursula Culpepper.

DENIS. That's all right. I'll put her off. She won't mind. Do come, Father.

MARK. I've got an engagement too.

DENIS. Couldn't you chuck it? I tell you what – let's dine at my club. The food's not up to much, but we can talk there

and not be disturbed. I'll just dash down and explain to
Ursula. You will come, won't you?

There is a pause.

MARK. I don't know, Denis. I don't know. I think probably
not.

DENIS (*cheerfully*). Well, I'll put Ursula off, anyway. Won't be
a second. (*Goes.*)

OSCAR, *who has watched the preceding scene without
stirring, looks at* MARK. MARK *answers the look. Then he
deliberately gets up and goes into the hall, reappearing in a
second with hat, gloves, and an overcoat.* OSCAR *helps him
on with his overcoat – still in silence. He starts slowly for the
hall.*

OSCAR. Mark?

MARK. Yes, Oscar?

OSCAR. What a loss to the Diplomatic that boy is going to be.

MARK. Loss? (*It has taken him a second to see what* OSCAR
means.) Now let me tell you, Oscar – if Denis thinks for one
moment I am going to countenance –

DENIS *reappears.*

DENIS. I've got a taxi, Father –

MARK (*turning on him angrily*). You realise, Denis, that this is
not going to be a very pleasant dinner for you – don't you?
I'm going to have a few very strong words to say to you
tonight –

DENIS. Yes, Father.

MARK. An actor, indeed! What in the name of heaven makes
you think you can be an actor?

DENIS. Oh. I don't know, Father. I just do. That's all.

MARK. Have you by any chance forgotten that one day you're
going to inherit my name?

DENIS. Well, I could always have a stage name, couldn't I, Father? I mean, after all, I suppose I could call myself Denis Wright.

Pause. OSCAR *throws his hands in the air.*

OSCAR. Complete breakthrough! Utter collapse along the entire front! Sue for terms, Mark – sue for terms.

MARK *advances on him belligerently.*

MARK. My God! Sometimes I feel like knocking you through a window.

OSCAR. All right. Why don't you?

MARK (*his voice strangled with fury*). Because – oh, because you're so bloody fat. (*He turns abruptly on* DENIS.) Now listen, Denis, if you think for one minute that you've got the faintest chance in the world of getting away with this arrant folly – you're making the biggest mistake of your young life –

As they reach the hall, the curtain has fallen.

ACT THREE

*The same. Time: 1950. The room once more has had a change
of character, and has reverted rather to its original bachelor
quality – though it gives the impression, here and there, of
having tried hard to make itself look like a love nest (1950
version) and of having failed to carry out its purpose through
being too well-bred.*

*It is about 6:30 of a winter evening and on the rise of the
curtain,* WILLIAMS *is discovered on the telephone. The dinner
table is laid for four places. The meal is evidently to be of
oysters only, and champagne. The radio can now be
distinguished as playing the 'Harry Lime' theme.*

WILLIAMS (*into telephone*). Sloane 7838? Cunliffe there? Oh,
   hullo, cock… It's me. Here's the yarn for tonight. Got a
   pencil?… Yes, you'll need it… Ready. (*Dictating slowly.*) I'm
   the hall porter at the Club… Yes… He's dining here – that's
   to say at the Club – with General Philipson… Yes, that's easy,
   it's what comes later… Got that? Okay… Dining at the Club
   with the General, going straight to Mr Denis's first night,
   where he's meeting Lord Bayswater and the Minister for
   War… War… After the theatre going to Lord Bayswater's for
   supper. Expect to be home about 12:30… Okay… Say one,
   it's safer… Tell me, how's Her Ladyship's cold? Better?…
   Oh, good… Got up this afternoon. Yes, I'll tell him. He'll be
   pleased. Okay. Now, have you got that straight? Okay, chum,
   that's it… Okay. Be seeing you. (*Rings off.*)

   DORIS *and* CHLOE *come in together, talking.* DORIS *is
   putting a latchkey away in her bag. Both girls are exquisitely
   dressed in evening gowns, and carry themselves like
   mannequins, which indeed they are.* DORIS *is the 1950
   edition of Sylvia.* CHLOE *is very beautiful and very
   statuesque.*

DORIS. So I said to Madam, I said, personally I never have thought an hour was enough at lunchtime and just because I'm ten minutes late it doesn't mean the whole dressmaking business is going to go bankrupt, does it? (*To* WILLIAMS.) Good evening, dear. This is Chloe – Mr Williams. She's at Fabia's too –

WILLIAMS (*to* CHLOE). How do you do, miss?

CHLOE. Good evening.

DORIS. Came along at a moment's notice – very kind of her I do think, just to make up the party, and she had a date with a gentleman, too –

CHLOE. No. With my mum.

DORIS. Oh, with your mum, was it, dear? How nice. (*To* WILLIAMS.) Neither of us have had a minute to do a thing to ourselves, as you know, dear, with Mr Wright ringing up like that at the last second. I'm sure we look positive frights –

WILLIAMS. Oh no, miss. You look as gorgeous as ever, and the other lady a fair treat, if I may say so. Pleasure to look at you both, I must say –

DORIS. Oh, but we just literally threw ourselves into our clothes, didn't we, dear?

CHLOE. Oh yes, dear. Just bundled ourselves in any old how – shocking it was.

DORIS, *as she speaks, is crossing the room with the slow, assured walk of the girl who is exquisitely dressed and knows it, and* CHLOE *as she speaks sits down with all the grace and dignity of a princess.*

DORIS (*inspecting the table*). Oysters. Do you like oysters, dear?

CHLOE. Not very in much, dear. Do you?

WILLIAMS (*to* CHLOE). Well, I'm very sorry, miss, but I'm afraid that's all there is. Just a little *bonne bouche* before the

theatre, as you might say. You'll be having supper
afterwards, of course –

CHLOE (*languidly*). Oh, well, of course – if that's all there is –

DORIS. What's that book you're reading, dear?

WILLIAMS. Trevelyan's *Social History*, miss.

DORIS. Why ever do you read that?

WILLIAMS. I find it very enjoyable, and most illuminating.
Well, I must be off. Going to see Mr Denis, too. This Old
Vic's a shocking place to get to.

DORIS. And who are you taking to the play?

WILLIAMS. Oh, no one, miss. You know me –

DORIS. You don't like ladies much, do you, dear?

WILLIAMS. I'm too old for ladies now, miss. I used to like 'em
once – in their place, of course.

DORIS. Oh. And what do you think is their place?

WILLIAMS *for reply, merely smiles.*

WILLIAMS. Well. Goodnight, ladies. Be good. (*Goes.*)

CHLOE (*languidly*). Whats the show we're going to see?

DORIS. It's *Julius Caesar*, I think, dear. You know –
Shakespeare.

CHLOE (*face falling*). Shakespeare? You didn't say that –

DORIS. Didn't I? Oh, well, I expect it'll be quite good. It often
is quite good, you know, Shakespeare. It's quite a surprise,
sometimes.

CHLOE. I didn't like the other one – that one Mr Wetherby took
us to –

DORIS. That wasn't Shakespeare, dear. It was quite modern,
Mr Wetherby was saying. He said the man who wrote it is
still alive. Fancy.

CHLOE. Of course it wasn't modern, silly. It was poetical. And they were all dressed up medieval –

DORIS. A play can be poetical and dressed up medieval and still be modern, dear, if it's by a man who's still alive.

CHLOE. Well, I didn't understand it anyway.

DORIS (*patiently*). Nor did I, dear. Not a bloody word. But that still doesn't make it Shakespeare, dear, does it –

CHLOE (*giving up*). Well, you might have told me it was Shakespeare tonight – I do think.

DORIS. I know you, dear. You'd have cried off. I told you it was Denis Wright –

CHLOE. Yes, but in *Julius Caesar*. (*A horrifying thought strikes her.*) Why, that's BC.

DORIS. I don't know why you always mind BC so much, dear. I think BC's quite pleasant, sometimes. Makes a nice change –

CHLOE. What part will Denis Wright be? Julius Caesar?

DORIS. No – I expect he'll be the one that says 'Friends, Romans, countrymen' –

CHLOE (*brightening a little*). Oh, is that in it? I know that. I'll look out for that. Mr Wright is Denis Wright's father, you said –

DORIS. That's it, dear. Mr Mark Wright. As a matter of fact he's Lord Binfield – really –

CHLOE. Oh!

DORIS. The British Ambassador in Paris.

CHLOE. Fancy!

DORIS. Don't let on you know, dear, will you – because the old chap does so like us all to think he's just Mr Wright –

CHLOE. Why?

DORIS. I don't know, really. I think quite a lot of gentlemen are rather like that. They'd think it terribly immoral to deceive their wives under their own names. Take another, and they'll be up to Lord knows what, and as gay and as innocent as sandboys –

CHLOE. Yes – but being an earl and an ambassador and all that, you'd think he wouldn't have a chance of getting away with another name, would you?

DORIS. Well, of course, dear, he hasn't. The number of times I've had to pretend to be blind, deaf, and half-witted, I can't tell you. Still, the old boy prefers it that way, and I wouldn't like to spoil his fun.

CHLOE. What's the other one like? This General?

DORIS. Oh, he's quite a nice old thing in his way. Quite harmless really. Oh, by the way, he likes to be known as Major Mason –

CHLOE. Why *Major*?

DORIS. He thinks it makes him sound younger. Sweet, isn't it?

CHLOE (*gloomily*). I don't think old gentlemen are ever sweet. I don't think I like old gentlemen at all.

DORIS. Old gentlemen are much nicer than young ones, they've got such lovely manners for one thing. I mean, with an old gentleman, for instance, a headache's a headache and no nonsense. My dear, I'm forgetting my manners now. Would you care to powder your nose?

CHLOE. Yes, I think that might be a good idea.

DORIS. This way, then, dear.

She sweeps majestically to the bedroom door, and holds it open for CHLOE.

CHLOE. Oh! What a very nice bedroom!

DORIS. Yes, it is quite nice really, isn't it? I mean, when you consider that it's really never used – This way, dear, on the right. (*Follows* CHLOE *out.*)

After a moment we hear male voices in the hall, and then
MARK *and* OSCAR *come in.* MARK *is now sixty-four, and*
OSCAR *sixty-seven. Both have worn quite well. They are in*
dinner jackets and overcoats. The latter they now proceed to
shed. OSCAR *with a certain amount of coughing and*
spluttering.

MARK. My dear chap, you never knew a single word of
Shakespeare… nothing but a common soldier… put your
coat down there… '*bleeding* piece of earth.' 'Oh, pardon me,
thou bleeding piece of earth' – not 'bloody piece of earth'.
You never could quote anything correctly.

OSCAR. It's 'bloody'. 'Oh, pardon me, thou bloody piece of – '
(*Stops in a fit of coughing.*)

MARK. Nonsense. I say, old chap, that cough of yours is rather
worrying, isn't it?

OSCAR. It doesn't worry me, so I don't know why on earth it
should worry you –

MARK. Are you sure you oughtn't to keep your coat on?

OSCAR. Quite sure –

MARK. I'll tell you what. I'll find you a rug –

OSCAR. If you think I'm going to dine on oysters and
champagne with two girls in a rug, you're off your head –

MARK. Mustn't take needless risks, though. We're none of us
quite as young as we were, you know.

OSCAR. What a damned idiotic remark! No, and we're none of
us quite as old as we're going to be either.

MARK. It's extraordinary how you get more crotchety and
more like a general every day –

OSCAR. And you get more cliché-ridden and more like an
ambassador. By the way – kindly remember I'm not a
general tonight – I'm a major.

MARK. My dear chap – I don't forget things of that kind. You
might be careful about my age too while you're about it.

OSCAR. What is it now?

MARK. Well – you don't need to be too specific. Middle fifties –

OSCAR. Ha!

MARK. You said something?

OSCAR. I said 'Ha'. What's young Denis going to be like?

MARK (*ponderously*). Well – now, Oscar – you know that I am not in anyway prone to exaggeration –

OSCAR. Do I?

MARK (*ignoring him*). And you know too that I have never been in any shape or form prejudiced by the mere fact that Denis happens to be my son.

OSCAR. Do I?

MARK. Nevertheless I am not, I think, making any ill-considered statement when I say that Denis's Mark Antony – without the slightest question – is the greatest I have seen since Irving.

OSCAR. You didn't see Irving.

MARK. How do you know I didn't?

OSCAR. Because he didn't play it.

MARK. Well, then, you didn't either, so shut up.

OSCAR (*a shade timorously*). What exactly are the plans for later?

MARK. Doris and I will be having a little supper here. I assumed you would be making rather similar arrangements.

OSCAR. Well, I've laid on a tentative little cold collation for two in my rooms.

MARK. Why tentative? Have you lost your nerve?

OSCAR (*sadly*). No. Just my youth.

MARK. Nonsense. 'Never say die' is my motto.

OSCAR. We may not say it, old chap – but quite soon we'll
have to do it.

MARK. Certainly. And, speaking for myself, when I do do it,
I'll look back on an exceptionally well-ordered and well-
conducted life. Or rather lives.

OSCAR. It beats me how you've got away with both of them all
these years.

MARK. Well. It doesn't beat me. I've got away with them for
precisely the reasons I've always told you I would get away
with them. Skill, application, finesse, and a superb talent for
organisation. You know, Oscar, I may well have stumbled on
the whole secret of successful living.

OSCAR. Hmm!

MARK. To divide the illicit from the domestic, the romantic
and dangerous from the dull and secure – to divide them into
two worlds and then to have the best of both of them. Years
ago in this very room you told me it couldn't be done – Well,
I've done it – not only here in London, but in Paris, in Rome,
in Stockholm, and in La Paz.

OSCAR. What are you in Paris? Monsieur Droit, *l'espion-
extraordinaire*?

MARK. No. Just Mr Wright, the English sculptor. A fourth-
floor studio in Montparnasse. A little model –

OSCAR. Called Mimi.

MARK. Albertine.

OSCAR. Dying of consumption?

MARK. No. Just an existentialist. Mr Wright is very happy in
Paris. And so, may I add, is Lord Binfield.

OSCAR. Luck! That's all it's been from the beginning. Luck
and nothing else.

MARK. I don't recognise the term.

OSCAR. But, my God – you take such appalling risks. Look at tonight, for instance –

MARK. Tonight? Tonight is an excellent example of my aptitude for planning. At the last minute I learn that my wife has influenza, and that the doctor has forbidden her to go out. What do I do? Quick as thought I ring up Charlie Bayswater, who I know is going to the theatre with his friend the War Minister, and make a date with him for five minutes before curtain up in the bar, where all the photographers will be floating around. Too good a catch to miss – the four of us. (*Triumphantly.*) In the *Tatler* to show my wife on Wednesday –

OSCAR. And the girls?

MARK. The girls have their explicit instructions. You and I, on leaving the bar and the photographers, will proceed to our seats – and there sitting right next to us will be the two ladies whom we happened to have met at the Dutch Embassy last Monday. Fancy that. The operation of having one's cake and eating it is so absurdly simple, if performed with the necessary attention to detail and organisation.

The telephone rings. He gets up to answer it.

(*Into telephone.*) Hullo… Hullo?… Who? (*His face shows acute alarm. In a badly disguised voice.*) Oh no, he's not 'ere. What nime shall I tell 'im… Yes, milady… Very good, milady… No, the General's not 'ere, neither… No, milady… No, I don't know, milady… (*Rings off. In a whisper.*) How in the name of heaven did she know this number?

OSCAR. The missus?

MARK *nods distractedly.*

MARK. Yes, she must still have your number in her book.

OSCAR. But dammit, she knows I haven't lived here for donkey's years. Anyway, the number's been changed.

MARK. Perhaps she's delirious –

OSCAR. Did she sound delirious?

MARK. No. But they never do. Do you think I ought to go back?

OSCAR. Why don't you ring up?

MARK. Yes. I will. Good gracious. The girls!

He is on his way to the telephone when the bedroom door opens and the two girls come out.

DORIS (*as she enters*). It's got the plunging neckline, but of course it's strictly 1950 – oh, hullo. You been here long, dear?

MARK. We didn't realise you were gossiping in there –

DORIS. My dear, you'd only got to shout out. Oh, Chloe, I don't think you've met Mr Wright, have you?

MARK. How do you do?

CHLOE. How do you do? Very honoured, I'm sure, to meet Denis Wright's father –

MARK. Once upon a time, you know, Denis Wright was known as my son. Now I'm known as his father – it's rather shaming, isn't it?

CHLOE. Shaming? What a quaint, old-fashioned word. I rather like it, don't you, Doris? Shaming?

DORIS. Yes, dear. This is General – er – Major Mason, dear. Do you remember I told you all about him –

OSCAR (*winningly*). Oh – not *all* about me, I hope. (*Laughs seductively, but it lapses into a wheezy cough.*)

MARK. The Major's got a slight cold, I'm afraid. Caught it out duck-shooting – didn't you, Major?

OSCAR. Yes. Gets a bit chilly, you know, out there in the marshes. Many chaps younger than myself go down with pneumonia, you know –

CHLOE. Well, it seems rather silly to do it then, doesn't it?

OSCAR. Ah, but then a cold is a small sacrifice to pay for the pleasures of an active life, don't you think?

CHLOE. No. I don't think I do. And I do hope you're not going to go giving your cold to me –

OSCAR. If you would allow me but the faintest chance of giving you anything, dear young lady, even my cold, I would count myself among the happiest of mortals –

MARK. Well now – shall we sit down?

DORIS (*sitting*). Come on, Chloe.

MARK. Come along, Major, lend a hand.

OSCAR. Yes, it would indeed be a pleasure to act as your Ganymede, dear lady.

CHLOE (*to* DORIS *in an undertone as she sits*). He talks so high-flown.

DORIS. They all do, dear. It's nice.

CHLOE. I don't think so. I think it's sort of – well – indecent.

OSCAR (*to* MARK) Well, why don't you slip out and ring her up?

MARK (*to* OSCAR*, in an undertone*). I'll ring up from the theatre. (*To the girls.*) Well, now, oysters. Doris and Chloe, if I may take that liberty –

CHLOE (*to* DORIS). What liberty?

DORIS (*in an undertone*). Saying Chloe, dear.

CHLOE. What's a liberty about that?

DORIS. Sh!

OSCAR *takes the vacant seat, coughing a little as he does so.*

MARK. Sure I can't get you a little covering for your shoulders, Major?

OSCAR. No, thank you, Wright. I wouldn't like the ladies to think I'm Whistler's mother.

DORIS *laughs gaily.*

DORIS. Oh, that's good, Major. That's very good. 'Whistler's mother'! Isn't that good, Chloe?

CHLOE (*mistiming it badly*). Yes. (*Laughs tinnily.*) Very good. Go on about what you said to Madam, dear.

MARK *meanwhile, has opened the champagne, while* OSCAR *sits, a neglected and forlorn figure, between the two girls.*

DORIS. Well – I said – after all, ten minutes isn't very much when you think that Princess Kasbak is a good half-hour late every day and Madam never says anything to her.

CHLOE. Do you know what I think Madam is? A snob. That's what Madam is. Anyway, she's not a Princess – not a real one.

DORIS. Well, I don't know dear, she does come from Anatolia.

CHLOE. I come from Pinner, but it doesn't make me a Countess. Besides, if she was a real princess she'd be at Hartnell's. (*Examining the champagne bottle as* MARK *pours.*) Oh, it isn't Bollinger?

MARK. No. It's Moet and Chandon '37. Would you rather have had Bollinger?

CHLOE. Oh, well – it doesn't really matter now you've poured.

MARK *passes on to* DORIS, OSCAR, *and himself.*

(*To* DORIS.) Yes, dear, I quite agree – Madam really is the limit. I mean, look at the way she treats Mr Claud and of course, Madam and Mr Freddy, well, I mean, we all know, don't we? And then again, dear, I've seen Madam sometimes –

MARK (*sitting and raising his glass*). Well, ladies. I'll just say – Here's to love!

DORIS *and* CHLOE (*murmuring*). To love.

They take a very perfunctory sip.

CHLOE (*to* DORIS). I mean, I've seen Madam simply furious with Mr Claud for no reason at all.

DORIS. Yes, dear. And what about that time when she made such a scene over that gold lamé?

CHLOE. Wasn't it a scream?

Both girls laugh gaily.

DORIS (*imitating Madam, apparently*). Pull those sleeves off! Pull those sleeves off, this instant!

CHLOE (*imitating Mr Claud, apparently*). Madam – you're breaking my heart. You're breaking my heart! Let go, Madam. Let go!

They laugh again. OSCAR talks to MARK across the table. As they converse, the girls are continuing their own discussion.

OSCAR. Do you get much golf these days?

MARK. No. Not much. An occasional round at St Cloud.

OSCAR. St Cloud? Yes, I've played there. It's quite a good course, isn't it?

MARK. Not bad. It plays rather short though –

OSCAR. I remember the ninth, I think. Isn't that the hole with the trees behind the green, and an enormous bunker on the right?

MARK. No. I think that's the eleventh you're thinking of –

OSCAR. Oh, the eleventh, is it? I thought it was the ninth.

Simultaneously, DORIS and CHLOE.

DORIS. Oh, it was a shame really, because it wasn't so bad, that dress. Do you remember it, dear, with that shaped bodice and the crinoline?

CHLOE. Oh yes, dear, I remember it very well. I thought it was quite unreasonable of Madam to go on like that –

DORIS. Well, of course, that's the trouble with Madam. I mean, she is unreasonable. I mean, look what she said to Gladys yesterday.

CHLOE. Oh, I didn't hear about that. What did she say?

DORIS. Oh, it was terrible. She said 'Get out,' she said, 'Get out – you're nothing but a… '

She lowers her voice to a whisper, happily inaudible to all but CHLOE. *The men have concluded their golfing conversation.*

CHLOE. She didn't!

DORIS. She did.

She repeats the three words, of which we can now tell that the middle one is 'little' and the last monosyllabic, necessitating a rounding of the lips. The first might he anything beginning with 'B'.

CHLOE. Oh – how dreadful.

DORIS. Unreasonable, you see. Just unreasonable.

She makes a face at CHLOE *significant of unreasonableness and then becomes conscious of her social duties.*

(*To* MARK.) Well, dear. How are you?

MARK. Oh, I'm very well, thank you, Doris.

DORIS. That's good.

MARK. And how are you?

DORIS. Oh, so-so, you know. I've got this headache again –

MARK (*gloomily*). Oh no!

Pause.

CHLOE. Funny – your saying that, Doris, because I've got an absolutely splitting headache.

DORIS. Oh, you poor thing! I am sorry.

OSCAR (*to* CHLOE). Where exactly is your headache, dear lady? Here? (*Touches her forehead.*)

CHLOE. Well – all over, really –

OSCAR. All over? Ah then, I've got exactly the thing for it. The very latest drug. I believe Mark and Doris are deserting us after the play, so if you would do me the honour of having a little supper with me at my flat, I could give it to you, then.

CHLOE. Oh. (*Faintly.*) How nice!

She makes a despairing face at DORIS *across the table.*

MARK (*at the window*). The car is there.

OSCAR (*looking at his watch*). We've got plenty of time. We've got well over half an hour.

MARK. I like to be early. Shall we leave the ladies, Major?

OSCAR *gets up, fails to make it first time, and sits down again.*

OSCAR. Funny thing – my knee caught the leg of the table.

He laughs jovially, the laugh once more becoming a cough.
MARK *comes to help him.*

MARK. Let me give you a hand.

OSCAR (*testily*). All right, all right. I can manage. (*Strikes out vigorously for the bedroom door.*) From the way he treats me sometimes, you'd think I was an old cripple, or something.

He laughs gaily, waves to the ladies, disappears, and we hear a crash as he enters the bedroom.

MARK (*alarmed*). Good heavens! Major! What have you done?

MARK *follows him into the bedroom.*

DORIS. You see, dear, what I say about old gentlemen is that they're so cosy. Cosy old ducks – that's what they are –

CHLOE (*plainly miserable*). Well, I don't think my one's cosy at all.

DORIS. Oh, he's really quite a dear, the General, when you get to know him.

CHLOE. I don't think I want to get to know him.

DORIS. You mustn't mind just because he talks high-flown, dear. I was telling you, they all talk high-flown –

CHLOE (*imitating*). 'If I might have the honour – dear lady – a little supper at my flat – I would count myself the happiest of mortals' – I mean, it's practically Lord Byron, isn't it?

DORIS. Well, I think that's nice, dear, don't you?

CHLOE. No. I think I want to go home.

DORIS. Oh, what a shame!

CHLOE. I shouldn't really have come out at all. I promised Mum I'd help her with the washing – and I could have got on with that jumper –

DORIS. Well, all right, dear, you go off. They won't mind. That's what's so nice about old gentlemen. They never mind anything –

The sound of old gentlemen's voices can be heard approaching the bedroom door.

Here they are. Don't you say anything, dear. I'll fix it.

MARK *and* OSCAR *come in.*

MARK (*as he enters*). But why ring up here, anyway? She thinks I'm at my Club. And how on earth could she possibly know the number –

OSCAR. Don't ask me, old chap.

MARK. Well, well. All ready?

DORIS. Oh dear – isn't it a shame? Chloe's been taken quite queer, quite suddenly.

MARK. Oh. I'm so sorry.

DORIS. She thinks it must have been a bad oyster, don't you, dear?

CHLOE. Yes. That's right, dear. A bad oyster.

MARK. It couldn't have been a bad oyster. These oysters came from my club –

DORIS. Poor Chloe! She feels she ought to go straight home, don't you, dear?

OSCAR. Oh, no.

CHLOE. Oh, yes. I must go home. Otherwise I might break out in a rash in the stalls, and that'd be terrible, wouldn't it?

DORIS. I'll drive her home, dear. Won't take me five minutes –

OSCAR. Look – let me drive her home.

CHLOE (*sharply*). Oh, no. (*Recovering herself.*) Oh, no, Major, please don't bother.

OSCAR (*winningly*). My dear young lady, I can assure you that the inestimable boon of prolonging our all too brief acquaintance by an extra five minutes would far outweigh the faintest element of bother –

CHLOE *stares at him, as if he were some particularly repulsive cobra, momentarily in the guise of Lord Byron. She gives a faint shudder and turns quickly to* MARK.

CHLOE. Well – it has been nice, Mr Wright. Perhaps you'll let me come again some time. Come on, Doris.

OSCAR (*advancing on her*). And how may I give myself the pleasure of a renewal of this encounter?

CHLOE (*helplessly*). Is it my phone number you want?

OSCAR. That would be a privilege indeed.

CHLOE. Well – you can always get me at Fabia's, except that Madam doesn't really like us being rung up in working hours – and I can't go upsetting Madam, can I? Because, you see, I'm really only there working hours. Come on, Doris.

She darts out. DORIS *lingers at the door.*

DORIS (*to* OSCAR). Don't worry, General. I'll fix things.
(*Follows* CHLOE *out.*)

OSCAR *shrugs his shoulders forlornly.*

MARK (*chuckling*). Poor old Oscar. What very bad luck.

OSCAR. I can't really see what you find so hilarious about
having poisoned one of your guests.

MARK (*laughing*). Nonsense. She's not poisoned, she's running
away from you, that's all.

OSCAR. There's no need for you to laugh. If I'm a joke, so are
you.

MARK. Joke? Speak for yourself.

OSCAR. I'm speaking for both of us. You know what we are,
Mark – just a couple of stock Punch figures for whom the
austerity age has no further use.

MARK. Nonsense, Oscar. It's got plenty of use. Even the
austerity age has to have generals and ambassadors.

OSCAR. Yes – but not my kind of general – nor your kind of
ambassador. Austerity generals – austerity ambassadors. My
God – you see them around everywhere – drinking dill water
and eating grated carrots and talking basic English. Heavens!
How I hate austerity, don't you?

MARK. I can't hate it. I represent it.

There is the noise of a stone against the window.

What was that?

OSCAR. Stone at the window.

There is another stone.

There it is again.

MARK *goes to the window.*

MARK. It's probably Doris. She must have forgotten her key –
(*Looking out.*) Doris?

CAROLINE (*off*). Mark!

MARK (*hurtles backwards into the room, speechless*). My God! My God! Oscar – my God!

OSCAR. What's the matter?

MARK. Caroline.

OSCAR (*rising*). It couldn't be!

MARK. It is. It is.

A woman's voice can be heard calling.

CAROLINE (*off*). Mark! Mark! Don't be so idiotic. Let me in.

MARK (*in a panic*). She's seen me. I'm lost.

OSCAR. Say it's my flat. We're dining here alone –

MARK. Doris will be back –

CAROLINE (*off*). I'm freezing out here, and I've got a cold anyway. Hurry up, Mark – for pity's sake –

OSCAR. I'll say Doris is my friend. Better let her in, Mark.

MARK (*keening softly*). Oh, my God! Oh, Oscar, how awful! (*Slowly approaches the window. Out of the window, in tones of exaggerated sangfroid.*) Hullo? Who is that? Oh, Caroline. What a surprise! I thought you were in bed.

CAROLINE (*off*). Well, I'm not, my dear. I'm out here. But I'll be in my coffin tomorrow if you don't let me in.

MARK (*with apparent surprise*). Let you in. Oh yes. (*Loudly to OSCAR.*) Oscar, Oscar, let Caroline into your flat. Just coming, Caroline.

OSCAR. Is she delirious?

MARK. She didn't seem to be –

OSCAR. I mean – she's not in her dressing gown or anything?

MARK. I didn't notice.

OSCAR. You must have noticed.

MARK. Go and let her in, Oscar.

OSCAR *goes out.* MARK, *left alone, rushes to try to remove traces of the two girls' presence. He is in the act of bundling plates into a drawer when the front door is heard opening.* CAROLINE *comes in, followed by* OSCAR. *She is an imposing old lady of decided beauty, dressed in an evening gown and a cloak.*

CAROLINE. Good evening, dear.

MARK. Good evening, Caroline. Oughtn't you to be in bed?

CAROLINE. I got up this afternoon because I had no temperature. I took it again at five and I still hadn't one, so I decided to come to the first night. You've given my seat to Charlie Bayswater, haven't you, dear?

MARK. Oh, yes, but he's chucked.

CAROLINE. How fortunate.

MARK. Very lucky you finding me here, Caroline – in Oscar's flat.

CAROLINE. Yes, dear. I rang up the Club and you weren't there.

MARK. As a matter of fact I was delayed at the Foreign Office and at the last possible moment a long dispatch came in –

CAROLINE. Not one of those complicated cyphers –

MARK. Very complicated, my dear –

CAROLINE. From Mesopotamia? Of course, it couldn't be – it's called something else now, isn't it?

OSCAR. I'm sorry you had to throw stones at my window. The trouble is, you can never hear the front doorbell here –

CAROLINE *is looking idly round the room.*

CAROLINE *(looking at wireless).* Oh, so that's where the little wireless went to. I've always wondered.

MARK. I – er – lent it to Oscar – I'm sorry. I should have told you.

OSCAR. Yes. It's been astonishingly useful. Astonishingly – six o'clock news –

CAROLINE. At twenty to, exactly, Denis said I could ring him up. What's the time now? Oh, the clock from the morning room. Nearly twenty-five to. But that clock always gains about three minutes a week, dear. Do you regulate it?

MARK. Do you?

OSCAR. Oh yes. Constantly. Charming present of Mark's, wasn't it?

CAROLINE. We've got seven and a half minutes. Have you ordered a car, darling?

MARK. Yes.

CAROLINE. Well, we'll send it away. I've brought the Daimler.

MARK. Oh, you have, my dear. That's splendid. (*In a whisper to* OSCAR.) Doris, Doris.

OSCAR. Oh – Caroline – by the way – a friend of mine is coming with us –

CAROLINE. Oh, yes. The Minister for War?

MARK. No, no. He chucked, too.

CAROLINE. What a lot of chucking.

MARK. Well, as a matter of fact, it's a lady, a friend of Oscar's.

CAROLINE. Oh. Mabel Brightlingsea? Dear old Mabel. Is she quite up to going out these days?

OSCAR. No. As a matter of fact, Caroline, I don't think you know her. It's just a young friend of mine – I thought I'd give her a treat, you know. (*Crossing to champagne.*) Well, now, Caroline, could I perhaps offer you a glass of champagne? It's Moet and Chandon '37 –

The flat door slams.

Here is the lady.

DORIS *enters.*

DORIS. Well, that's done. I hope I haven't made you late, Major.

CAROLINE. Doris, isn't this nice. I'm coming to the first night with you.

DORIS (*turning and seeing* CAROLINE). Oh!

CAROLINE. Yes, my temperature went down and I got up. This is the dress you showed me at Fabia's. How do you like it in white?

DORIS. Oh, it's lovely.

CAROLINE. Isn't it nice I am able to wear it for the first night, after all. And I hear there's still a seat.

DORIS. Yes. Chloe's.

CAROLINE. Chloe?

DORIS. That's the tall girl I told you I thought the General would like to meet, do you remember?

CAROLINE. Oh, yes.

DORIS. Well, she got taken quite queer – a bad oyster, it was – and so it'll be just the four of us – which will be ever so nice, won't it? And nice for Denis, too, having his Mum and Dad out front after all.

CAROLINE. Are you ready to start, dear?

DORIS. No. I'll just fix my hair, won't be a tick. (*Goes into the bedroom.*)

CAROLINE. What a sweet girl that is. So much nicer than that horrid existentialist, in Paris.

MARK (*groaning*). Caroline! Caroline! Caroline!

CAROLINE. Yes, my dear?

MARK. You have shocked and blasted me to the very depths of my being.

CAROLINE. Have I, my dear? I do apologise. I would have avoided it if I possibly could – but after you went blithering away on the telephone just now about: 'I don't know where he is, milady' – darling, what a cockney accent – really – I realised I'd have to take drastic action if I wanted to see Denis play Mark Antony tonight.

MARK. How long have you known, how long?

CAROLINE. Now, let me see. (*To* OSCAR.) When was it that Oscar first let his flat to a Mr Mark Wright. That's quite a long time ago now, isn't it, dear?

OSCAR. Thirty-three years ago, only thirty-three years.

CAROLINE. Is it really? How time flies, to be sure. Well, now, when bills started turning up on my desk for decorations to No. 12 Wilbraham Terrace –

MARK. Oh, my God!

CAROLINE. And letters addressed to Mr Mark Wright – darling, I do hope you're not as careless with confidential documents at the Embassy as you are with letters addressed to Mr Mark Wright.

MARK. I told you Mark Wright was an old friend of mine –

CAROLINE. You told me lots of things, dear, and you took the greatest trouble to make me believe them. If you tell lies to Foreign Ministers as clumsily as you tell them to me, I wonder that anyone ever speaks to us at the United Nations.

OSCAR. Oh, what a tangled web we weave –

CAROLINE. No, not a very tangled web, a remarkably simple web on the whole. And when – to crown it all, you go and choose a girl from a shop where I get my dresses and, of course, pick the very one whom I know particularly well –

MARK. Doris never, never mentioned a word.

CAROLINE. Of course not, dear. I swore her to utter secrecy – and she's a sweet girl, so I knew she would never give me away.

MARK. Caroline, for thirty-three years you have been deceiving me. You have just made the most immoral and unprincipled statement it has ever been my lot to listen to.

CAROLINE. Is it immoral and unprincipled? What do you think, Oscar?

OSCAR. I'm afraid, Caroline, that I must tell you that I am as deeply shocked as Mark.

CAROLINE. Oh, well, then perhaps I *am* unprincipled and immoral. You see, I've never been much tempted to the more conventional forms of immorality – though I admit – now I come to think of it – that on just a couple of occasions it might have been rather nice to have been Caroline Wright –

MARK (*aghast*). Oh – Caroline!

CAROLINE. But I never did, dear. I never did.

MARK. That, at least, is something.

CAROLINE (*brightly*). So as I've never been immoral in other ways, this immorality of mine in not ever having made an issue of Mr Mark Wright was really only, I suppose, what you might call – having my little fling.

MARK. Well, Oscar, I ask you –

CAROLINE. I nearly made an issue once, you know, over that first girl – that silly flapper – what was her name? Mark, what was her name?

MARK *doesn't reply.*

Oscar – that silly girl he met on a bus – Daphne Prentice, that was it.

MARK *groans.*

Yes. I nearly made an issue over her. But then I thought – well, if I do – he'll drop this silly girl all right, but he'll hate me for ever afterwards. So what's the use? And then there was that time when you were thinking of leaving the Diplomatic because of that creature – what was her name now – Nora Patterson – and what an issue I'd have made over that – but then suddenly you dropped the whole idea – and I breathed again –

MARK. Ah. Denis told you that, I suppose?

CAROLINE (*puzzled*). Denis? Mark – you don't mean it was Denis who got you to change your mind on that? Oh – I knew of course, you wouldn't have done it yourself – but I always imagined it was Oscar who rescued you. It was Denis, was it? (*Fondly.*) Oh, what a clever boy, and he never even told his mother!

MARK. This is my wife, Oscar. This is the woman I have always looked up to as a pillar of rectitude and simple-heartedness.

CAROLINE. Simple-heartedness doesn't mean half-wittedness, dear. Anyway I made no issue over Nora Patterson, because I didn't have to after all – and none of the myriad others have really bothered me –

MARK (*groaning*). What!

CAROLINE. You see, from the beginning I thought to myself – well, this Mark Wright business must go rather deep. I'm his wife, and if he really wants to change his identity from time to time, then it must, in some way, be my fault. Something that I can't give him, that he wants and can find elsewhere. I would have liked to have been Mrs Mark Wright, but I knew I couldn't be. I knew I couldn't ever be anything more than the wife of Mark Binfield – and as I wanted, more than most things, to go on being that, I realised I had to give up all claims on Mark Wright. And I did. Except, of course, that I had to do my best to see that Mr Wright came to no harm. In Paris, for instance, we always have to have him followed by the Embassy detectives. (*To* OSCAR.) He will go to such dreadful dives in Montparnasse.

MARK *groans again and covers his face with his hands.* CAROLINE *looks at her watch.*

Right. Time to ring up Denis. Oscar, get the number, will you? It's Waterloo 6849.

OSCAR *goes to the telephone.*

Darling, I am feeling so nervous for Denis tonight. How nice that you will be there to hold my hand. Darling, why will you wear stiff collars with your dinner jacket. It looks so old-fashioned.

MARK *groans for the last time.* CAROLINE *squeezes his hand.*

OSCAR (*into telephone*). Oh, stage door... would you put me through to Mr Wright... it's his mother.

CAROLINE *gets up and goes to the telephone.* OSCAR *comes to* MARK, *who is still sunk gloomily in his chair.*

CAROLINE (*into telephone*). Denis?... Darling, just to wish you everything in the world... yes, I'm coming. No, I am much better...

OSCAR. The best of both worlds? How easy if you have the genius for it –

MARK. Oh, Oscar. The shame of it! The shame!

CAROLINE (*into telephone*). Oh, darling, how sweet of you. Yes, of course, we'd love it. (*To* MARK.) He's chucking his first-night party and asking us to supper afterwards. Isn't that nice? (*Into telephone.*) Darling, how do you feel?

MARK *rises.*

Don't worry, you'll be splendid. Well, darling boy, everything in the world. Here's Father.

She hands the telephone to MARK, *who takes it in a daze.*

DORIS (*entering*). Is my hair all right?

MARK (*into telephone*). Denis?... Yes. Just to wish you the very best of luck, old chap... Well, as a matter of fact, I've just been saying to Oscar that I consider it the best Mark Antony I have seen... (*Catches* OSCAR's *eye.*) since Tree...

OSCAR (*in a whisper*). Ask him about 'bloody'.

MARK. Shut up. (*Into telephone.*) What, old chap... Mother? Yes, I knew you'd be glad...

OSCAR (*louder*). Ask him about 'bloody' –

MARK. Go away. (*Into telephone.*) Oh, it's only your Uncle Oscar. Some ridiculous idea he has that it's 'bloody piece of earth', and not 'bleeding...' (*To* OSCAR.) There you are, you see. You've gone and put him off. He says he can't remember himself now –

OSCAR. Oh, Lord. (*Snatches the telephone. Frantically into telephone.*) Look, old chap, it doesn't matter, you know. Just say the first thing that comes into your head – bloody or bleeding – it doesn't matter, old chap. It really doesn't –

MARK *snatches the telephone back.*

MARK. Pay no attention to him, Denis. He's drunk... Well, won't keep you, old chap. All the very best –

DORIS. Give him mine, too –

MARK. Oh, and Doris sends her love too... No, Denis, there's no point in lowering your voice and being tactful. I haven't made a bloomer... Yes, well, it's a long story. I'll tell you later. (*Rings off.*)

CAROLINE. Come on, now. We're going to be late. Oscar, will you escort Doris to the car? Where's my bag?

DORIS. Come along, Major, you must look after me tonight.

OSCAR. That will be a pleasure, my dear.

DORIS. We might do a little dancing later.

DORIS *and* OSCAR *go out.*

CAROLINE (*running her finger on top of the radio*). Really. I must speak to Williams about the way he keeps this flat.

MARK (*hopelessly*). You must speak to Williams.

CAROLINE. I have a little confession to make about Williams, darling. With the servant problem so terrible, it did seem such a waste – so he does occasionally pop in to Belgrave Square, and help out. Just now and then, you know.

MARK. Just now and then?

CAROLINE. I knew you wouldn't mind.

MARK. You knew I wouldn't mind?

She inspects the bronze head of Sylvia.

CAROLINE. What a very pretty face Sylvia did have. Do you know, dear, she still looks a little like that.

MARK. What?

CAROLINE. Of course, she's quite old now. What would she be exactly? A year younger than you, isn't she? Sixty-three. Yes. She looks all of sixty-three, I'm afraid.

MARK (*aghast*). You mean – you know her?

CAROLINE. Sylvia Willoughby-Grant? My dear, we play bridge together.

MARK (*laughing hysterically*). No. No – not that! No, Caroline – you can't pull that one on me. She's in South Africa –

CAROLINE. My dear, didn't you know? She came back years ago – before the war. She lives in Chester Square. I tell you what would be rather nice. I'll have her to dinner next week –

MARK. Oh, God!

CAROLINE. She really looks quite sweet, you know. It'll really be such fun for you to meet her again after all these years, won't it?

MARK. Caroline, you wicked, wicked woman. I give in. Unconditional surrender. Sylvia now goes the way of Mark Wright –

CAROLINE. Well, darling, in a way I suppose that's only just, isn't it – seeing that up to now it's been Mark Wright that's always gone the way of Sylvia.

OSCAR *comes back with his overcoat on, and carrying* MARK*'s.*

All right, all right, Oscar, we're coming. Don't look so dejected, dear. You'll like her very much, I know, when you meet her. A very sweet and charming old lady.

She smiles at him. After a pause he smiles back. She goes out.

OSCAR (*as he helps* MARK *on with his overcoat*). What does it feel like to grow from seventeen to sixty-four in five minutes? Having your cake and eating it, eh? (*Chuckles.*)

MARK. Well – all I can say is this. I have jolly well had my cake and I have jolly well eaten it – and that's more than can jolly well be said for most people, including yourself, so yah!

OSCAR. A little prep school, wasn't it, for an ambassador?

MARK. That wasn't an ambassador speaking. That was the last recorded utterance of Mr Mark Wright. (*Looking round room.*) Pity. It was fun. Oh, well, never say die, I suppose.

They move towards doors. OSCAR *turns off lights.*

Come on, Oscar.

They go out into the hall together.

Curtain.

The End.

DUOLOGUE

Duologue was first performed as *All On Her Own* on BBC2, on 25 September 1968, with the following cast:

ROSEMARY	Margaret Leighton
JOAN	Nora Gordon
Producer	Hal Burton
Designer	Stephan Paczai

Duologue was first performed on stage as *All On Her Own* at the Overground Theatre, Kingston, Surrey, in October 1974, with the following cast:

ROSEMARY	Margaret Stallard
Director	Maria Riccio Bryce

Duologue was first performed at the King's Head Theatre, London, in a double bill with *The Browning Version*, on 21 February 1976, with the following cast:

ROSEMARY HODGE	Barbara Jefford
Producer	Stewart Trotter
Designer	Geoff Stephens

Characters

ROSEMARY HODGE

Setting

Time: The present. Towards midnight.

Place: A house in Hampstead, London.

The stage is in darkness. There is the sound of a car drawing up, the engine continuing to tick over.

ROSEMARY (*unseen*).

Thank you so much. I do hope I didn't take you too far out of your way... Yes, it is rather a nice house, I have to admit. No, a little earlier. William and Mary. Far too big, of course, for these days. My late husband chose it. He was an architect, you see, and fell in love with it. Are you quite sure I can't tempt you inside for a drink? It's still quite early. Oh, is it as late as that? I quite understand. See you at the Joynson-Smythes' on Thursday, then. Goodnight. (*Calling again.*) Oh, thank you for the book. My favourite subject. I can't wait to read it.

The car drives away. Silence. Lights are suddenly switched on in an empty room which, although we may only see part of it, is plainly a large 'salon', decorated carefully according to the period. Visible to us and necessary for the action is an armchair, a sofa centre-stage, a fireplace on which is an antique pendulum clock, and a door through which ROSEMARY *has just entered. She is carrying a book which, if we can make out its title, is called* Guilt and the Human Psyche: A Study of Contemporary Literature. *She puts the book down by an armchair and pours herself a fairly hefty drink. Then she sits with it, puts it down on a table after a thirsty gulp, and picks up the book, riffling its pages quickly before throwing it down impatiently and picking up another, plainly a Crime Club selection. This too she puts down as she takes another gulp of her drink, and then stares at the sofa for a long time.*

What time did you die?

She has spoken conversationally, as if to a person sitting close to her in the room.

Gregory, what time did you die? Wasn't it about now? The police said you'd been dead between eight and nine hours, and it was eight in the morning Mrs Avon found you over there, on that sofa.

She stares at the sofa which is very tidy and clean, not looking in the least as though someone had once been found dead on it.

Or just before. Yes, it must have been before, because when she called me down the clock was striking. It's one of those silly things you remember. So it must have been about now you died.

The clock gently and musically strikes the half-hour.

A woman at a party I've just been to told me quite seriously that she talks to her husband every night at exactly the hour he died. He sends her long messages on a Ouija board or something. Well, I haven't got a Ouija board, but I'm talking to you Gregory, and at near enough the time you died. You might just answer, you never know, and then I'll have a story to tell at a party, too. God, the party I've just been to. How you'd have hated it. *Hated* it. A young man reading a paper on Kafka and a discussion afterwards. You wouldn't even have known who Kafka was, would you?

(*In a warm, broad North Country accent.*) Kafka? Is that a new government department, love?... Oh a writer, was he? Fancy.

(*In her own voice.*) You'd have tried to steal off home before the discussion, and I wouldn't have let you, and you'd have gone off quietly to a corner of the room and got yourself quietly whistled. No, that wasn't your word.

She gets up and pours herself another drink.

Gregory, what *was* your word?

Silence.

Something revolting. Yes. You'd have got yourself quietly drunk and wouldn't have noticed my triumph in the discussion when I said to this young man: 'You see, Mr Whosit, Kafka strikes no chord on my piano. I'm afraid I don't believe in nameless fears. I believe that all fears can be named and once named can be exorcised.' Rather good. It got applause. Nice if it had been true.

She goes back to her seat.

'Are you sure you can name all your fears, Mrs Hodge?'… This was the hostess… 'Surely when you're alone at night in that great house of yours, Mrs Hodge, when your boys are away at school, you must sometimes have disquieting thoughts? I mean lonely widows usually – '

(*Sharply.*) 'Loneliness is a defeat, Mrs Ponsonby. I have far too many things to occupy my mind ever to feel lonely. I despise loneliness. I despise middle-aged women who talk to themselves at dead of night.'

She takes a long drink.

But I'm not talking to myself. I'm talking to you, Gregory, aren't I? Talking to a dead you.

She laughs.

Well, talking to a live you wasn't very different. It was still talking to myself. I hope you didn't hear that because it was rude and I was never rude to you in all our married life, was I? Unfailingly polite – wasn't it 'unfailingly' you used to say, or 'invariably'?… No. 'Unfailingly'. Poor Gregory – how you hated that, didn't you? How you longed for just one honest, vulgar, hammer-and-tongs, husband-and-wifely flamer! But I never gave it to you, did I? I was brought up to be polite, you see – unfailingly polite. Was that so wrong?

(*Answering herself.*) Yes, it was. It was pretty damn bloody!

(*Surprised.*) Do you know – talking to you is rather good for me, Gregory. I should do it more often. It might even make me honest.

She takes another sip of her drink, then again looks over at the sofa.

I called you an architect again tonight, Gregory. I even said it was you who chose this house. That's a laugh considering how you hated it. I call you an architect all the time, now that you're no longer there to deny it.

(*In Gregory's North Country accent.*) Why do you call me what I never was, Rosemary, and never could have been? You make me feel as if I'd wasted all my life. I was a builder and proud of it. I despise bloody architects. They're always so busy concealing lavatory pipes they forget they've got to flush.

(*In her own voice.*) Yes. You beat me on that, Gregory. The only real battle I suppose you ever won. To stop you talking about lavatories all over Hampstead, and making people think I was married to a plumber, we settled on 'builder'. Well, 'building contractor'. It sounded better.

She goes to get another drink.

All right. I'm being honest with you, Gregory. Now you be honest with me.

Drink in hand, she stands over the sofa looking down at it.

Tell me if the police and the coroner and the insurance people were right when they said it was a drunken accident? Or if I'm right now when I say you killed yourself?

Silence. ROSEMARY, *as if consciously committing a blasphemous act, stretches herself out on the sofa.*

(*In his accent.*) But Rosemary, darling, why should I kill myself? I had everything to live for, hadn't I? I'd just sold my business in Huddersfield for a lot of money, and bought a beautiful house in Hampstead, and for the first time in my life could enjoy all the ease and comfort of a charming, civilised, cultured retirement in London, with my charming, civilised, cultured wife beside me, and my two charming, civilised, cultured sons at Eton. And my wife is still quite young, you know, as wives go, and still quite attractive in her way – well, I find her so anyway, but I suppose you'd say I was prejudiced about that and always have been. Oh, yes. I was a lucky man when I was alive. There's no doubt about it. Why on earth should I have killed myself?

She gets up from the sofa and goes back to her chair.

(*In her own voice.*) If I answered that for you, Gregory, would you still tell me whether you did?

After a pause.

Of course you wouldn't.

(*In Gregory's voice.*) But all that happened that night, Rosemary darling, was that after we had that little tiff about whether I couldn't go out on the town with Alf Fairlie from the rugger club instead of going with you to the ballet – which I never did fancy very much, as you know – along with the Fergusons who always treated me like some kind of nit who'd married a mile above myself. Not the only ones to do that, down here in Hampstead, come to that, which doesn't always seem to put you out too much, Rosemary love – be honest now, does it? Is that why we're in Hampstead? Is it – to show me my place?

(*Stridently, in her own voice.*) On, my God! That wasn't me. I'm not as honest as that, am I? Gregory, that must have been you! Gregory, are you in this room?

(*Looking around anxiously.*) Are you in this room, Gregory?

(*More loudly.*) Are you?

There is no answer and no sign. ROSEMARY *swallows her drink and pours another.*

Let's try again!

(*In North Country accent again.*) Well, we had this little argie-bargie, love – remember? And afterwards, you went up to bed – never a cross word, mind you – impeccably polite as.

(*In her own voice, excitement mounting.*) It was 'impeccably', not 'unfailingly' or 'invariably'. No, it wasn't – it wasn't – but it *was* just then. Gregory, you *are* here! You are, aren't you? You're here, with me, in this room?

Again there is no answer and no sign.

(*Controlling herself.*) Go on. Go on, Gregory!

She begins to speak again, with a conscious imitation of his accent, carefully contrived at first – as in the two previous 'Gregory' speeches – and only later does her voice quite suddenly seem to become a spontaneous expression of a living personality.

All right, Rosemary darling, it was like this. You went up to bed, see, impeccably polite.

(*In her own voice.*) That was me that time, not you!

(*In his voice.*) ... as always, and it was early still – not more than nine o'clock or thereabouts, and so I'm afraid, love, I got myself at that decanter that you're holding now.

(*Very gently.*) Going my way, are you, love?

ROSEMARY *slams the decanter down as if she had hardly known she had it in her hand.*

Careful of the whiskey, love. It's bad stuff for widows living on their own. You had two before you went to the party. Not many there, I shouldn't think, knowing those parties – had Algerian burgundy, I expect – but you probably sneaked yourself an extra glass or so, shouldn't be surprised. And now three since eleven twenty-five.

ROSEMARY *pours some of her drink back into the decanter.*

That's better, Rosemary darling. Can't be too careful, I always say. Look what happened to me that night.

ROSEMARY, *with an effort at control, pours water into her drink and then, as if shrugging off Gregory's presence, deliberately adds to it from the decanter.*

(*Still in Gregory's voice.*) Think it's not me talking to you? Think it's just you talking to yourself?

(*In her own voice.*) I know it's just me talking to myself – in a bad Huddersfield accent.

(*In his voice.*) I didn't talk in a Huddersfield accent, love. I was born in Newcastle.

(*Sharply, in her own voice.*) Did I know that? Yes, of course, I must have.

(*Controlled.*) All right, Gregory. What happened to you that night? Tell me.

There is a pause, as if she really were expecting a reply. Then, she laughs.

Of course! The game is – I begin and then you take over.

(*In his voice.*) Well, Rosemary darling, you'd gone to bed, as I told you, and I got at the decanter and got myself fairly whistled.

(*In her own voice.*) No, 'whoozled'. That was your word. You got yourself *'whoozled'*.

(*Unconsciously, in his voice.*) Aren't you going to say 'I wish you wouldn't use that *awful* expression, Gregory! If you mean 'drunk', why don't you say 'drunk'?

(*In her own voice, now stiff with fear.*) Because you weren't drunk. When you came up to my room you were quite sober. If you hadn't been, I'd have smelled it on your breath. I'd had enough experience of it these last fifteen years.

(*In his voice.*) But not much these last ten years, eh, love? Not from very close. And not at all that night.

(*In her voice.*) You said you wanted to sleep down here. And I told you to please yourself.

(*In his voice.*) Aye, you did. And I pleased myself. It was then, if you want to know, that I got myself really whoozled. Boy, did I get whoozled!

(*After a pause; in her own voice.*) You expected to come to bed?

(*In his voice.*) Not expected. Hoped, you might say. I'd say I was sorry, hadn't I?

ROSEMARY *nods.*

And it was a Friday night, after all. I know it wasn't back at Huddersfield, not working on Saturday and all – not working *any* bloody day down here! And I know things like that had, well – lapsed a bit lately between us – but, well, it's always a good way to make-up a quarrel, isn't it?

ROSEMARY *nods again.*

Don't cry, love. There's no need for that now. I told you, I didn't expect. I only hoped.

(*After a long pause; in her own voice.*) What about those pills?

(*In his voice.*) Well, this sofa isn't much of a place to sleep on, you know. A man my size.

ROSEMARY's *gaze is fixed on the sofa.*

Oh, very aesthetical, and quite the rage in North London, I don't doubt, but not too comfy for a man in a bit of a state. Whoozled, I know, but still in quite a state what with one thing and another. So I went up to the bathroom –

The immediate impression is that ROSEMARY *is listening intently, although of course she continues to speak.*

– and I found that bottle of pills that you use. Nembutal or some such name. Little yellow things. And I gave myself enough to make myself sleep – just two or three .

(*Interrupting herself; quietly.*) Six.

(*After a pause; in his voice.*) Was it six? I told you I was whoozled, didn't I? Well, doesn't that show it was an accident, love? I mean, if I'd wanted to kill myself I'd have taken sixteen, wouldn't I?

There is a pause. Then ROSEMARY *finishes her drink and shrugs hopelessly.*

(*In her own voice.*) Not if you wanted me to think it *was* an accident. And to let me have the money from the insurance.

(*With a sudden access of real grief.*) Oh, my God, do you think that money could make up for you? Oh, you bloody, bloody fool!

A moment.

But how were you to know?

She goes to replenish her drink.

Yes! Another whiskey. It'll be the last. Oh, Gregory, why did you do it? It's silly to ask you that, isn't it? I know why you did it – if you did it. Did you? No, what's the point! It'll only be my own brain answering for you again, and my brain will go on thinking no, and believing yes – yes and no, no and – until the end of time.

After taking a gulp of her drink.

And when will that be, Gregory? Are you allowed to know these things? And would you tell me if you were?

A moment.

No, you'd never say anything to hurt me, would you?

She looks round the room in silence for a moment.

It doesn't matter. Yes, I'm lonely, Gregory, and I do miss you. Quite terribly I miss you. Does that surprise you? I expect it does. It certainly surprised me.

She finishes her drink.

So you had everything to live for, did you? Your work, which you loved, finished by me. All your friends lost, and your life uprooted – by me. Your children, whom you loved, and who could have loved you, made to despise you – by me. And a wife – 'unfailingly polite' – who only knew she loved you when you were dead. And whom you loved and went on loving in spite of – I can say it. Oh yes, I'm brave enough! In spite of her driving you to your death.

(*Raising her voice for the first time.*) I did, Gregory, didn't I? I want the real truth now, and I'm not going to answer for you any longer through my brain and with my voice! You'll have to find some other way. Open a door, break a window, upset a table! Make some sign! But do something, and tell me the real truth! Did I kill you?

Nothing stirs in the room and there is no sound.

I killed you, didn't I? Say it, Gregory – say it!

The clock quietly and musically begins to strike midnight. There is no other sound. ROSEMARY *waits until it is finished, then goes quietly round the room, turning off the lights. The last light left burning is by the sofa. Just before she turns it off, she gently puts her hand on the part where Gregory's head might, one night, have lain. Then she looks round and sees the decanter still half-full. After the briefest hesitation she picks it up and takes it with her as she turns off the light and goes out. A light seems to linger on the sofa before final complete and silent darkness.*

Curtain.

The End.